Tumbling Dreams

April Adams

Published by Lechner Syndications

www.lechnersyndications.com

ISBN 13: 978-0-9918164-8-4

"If you are afraid of failure, you don't deserve success."

- Nastia Liukin

.

CONTENTS

APRIL ADAMS

INTRO

Nadia free-jumped off the ground and landed on the bar in a cross split. Her legs touched firm leather and everything felt right with the world.

She was calm, centered, a champion.

Her perfect posture and golden-brown eyes radiated confidence, as always. Her short, chestnut-brown hair was carefully pinned back with a fuchsia-and- silver clip to match her leotard—her team colors. She imagined waving calmly from the podium, a gold medal adorning her slender neck.

Nadia quickly transitioned into two flying flank circles followed by a flair, winging her strong straight legs around her body like a break-dancer. She followed the flair with a series of hip circles off the side of the beam.

Starting from a straddle, Nadia extended her body backwards and lifted her legs up into a handstand. With a delicate twist and leap, she popped upright, standing balanced on the narrow leather bar.

Cake, she thought. *Nothing better than this.*

In the background, "Nadia's theme" played. The song had been used as the soundtrack for a montage of Romanian gymnast Nadia Comaneci's best routines during the 1976 Summer Olympics. She'd never used it for her floor routine, but it had become her anthem.

Nadia thought of it as her anthem, as well. Rather than distract her, the song lifted her spirits making her feel sure she was going to out-do her personal best.

Arching her body backwards, Nadia performed an aerial walkover, one leg tumbling over after the other, and followed it up with two scissor leaps and an arabesque.

Scissor leaps required an incredible amount of balance and strength because she had to change the position of her legs in mid-air. But Nadia had been doing them for at least three years. Her feet easily found the bar every time.

Each of her moves was crisp and precise, just like her mom had taught her.

And they call Sara, Tree Frog? Nadia thought. *I'm the one who never falls off.*

The compulsory components for Regionals weren't much harder than they'd been for State finals the week before. Nadia already had most of them worked into her routine.

A series of two tumbling elements, at least one with flight? *Check.*

A dance series with at least two elements, one of which is a leap or jump requiring 180° split? *Got it.*

A full turn? *In my sleep.*

And a dismount of at least A value? *Try D.*

Nadia had been born for this. The daughter of a gymnast, she'd been named after gymnastics elite, Nadia Comanecii. And though tons of gymnasts had come and conquered since 1976, Comaneci was still Nadia's inspiration.

Nadia did a backward roll and pressed into a handstand.

Not hard enough, she thought. *I can do better.*

She jumped backwards with a half twist to walkover forward with step-out followed by a few dance steps and an aerial cartwheel. They were D-level moves. And Nadia's execution was exceptional.

My mom could do a tuck back salto with full twist at my age, Nadia thought, *and that's F-value.*

Bending deep in the knees for power, Nadia leapt backwards with her legs and arms tucked in. At full height, she bent her body into a twist and landed with her arms up in the air, one foot right behind the other. No wobbles.

Hmmm, Nadia thought. *Guess I can do it, too. I'm going home from*

2

Regionals with gold.

Concentrating hard, Nadia took a cleansing breath to prepare for her dismount. It was inspired by Gabby Douglas's 2012 Olympic routine. Arching her body backwards, Nadia did two back somersaults on the beam, then lifted off, bending her body in half into a pike.

She completed two more somersaults in the air and landed with her feet together, knees bent to absorb the impact.

Perfect.

Absolutely perfect.

Nadia pouted and shook her head in disbelief. She just didn't get.

"Your acrobatic skills are exceptional, Nadia," her mom said. She'd been watching Nadia perform from the basement staircase.

When Nadia was just a little girl, her mom had set up a regulation practice beam in their basement complete with crash mats and springboard. Nadia could just about clear her moves without wonking her head on the ceiling.

When she was teeny tiny, the bar was lower and her friends used to come over and pretend they were flying to Oz on it. Nadia had always thought it was cool, but lately she wondered if it was a bit much.

"You can run through this routine a million times," her mother continued, "and the outcome will always be the same. You have high start values on all your acro moves and you perform at or above expectations. You excel on beam, Nadia."

"Then why did I come in second at State?" Nadia challenged.

"You know why."

Nadia glared at her mother.

Frustrated, she huffed and flopped onto their old beat-up basement sofa. She picked up the remote control and hit "ON", glaring at Gabrielle Douglas's gold-medal-winning beam performance. Her form was perfect, but she also had a grace, a fluidity. There was something so beautiful about it. So natural.

It was breathtaking.

And it was that *thing*—that undefinable *something*-- that Nadia didn't have. Had never had.

"Artistry," Nadia said petulantly, "I don't have artistry. It's not a skill you can learn like a handspring or a pirouette. It's…it's…simply not my personality."

"I have something I think may help." Her mother smiled mischievously and ran upstairs. She came back down carrying a bottle of water and a DVD.

Nadia took the DVD and read the package. A sick feeling rose up from her stomach into her throat.

"I'm going to vomit," she said as she skimmed the package.

"The USAG educational Jr. Olympic Dance Workout Program?" Nadia read aloud. "Guaranteed to provide proper dance training for gymnasts at levels one through five. Are you kidding me?"

She tossed the DVD onto the couch beside her, too disgusted to even look at it.

"Next thing you know, you'll be signing me up for a soccer team. Oh! Or how about flamenco dancing? They do that twisty thing with their wrists. How about that?"

"That's a thought," said her mother, clearly amused.

Nadia lifted herself upright, head high, as if deeply offended.

"I'm glad you think this is funny," Nadia snapped. "What I really need is a more complicated mount, like a round-off jump with a half turn to back hip circle or a…a…round-off, flic flac with full twist. My start value is too low. I've got to bring it higher." She picked up a fact sheet she'd printed off the official USA Gymnastics website.

"The most difficult of the required elements are—"

Her mother shushed her with a warning glare.

Nadia's mother stroked her daughter's chestnut hair and wondered how long ago her beautiful face had frozen into such a deep scowl.

"If that's how you feel about it, Nadia," she said. "By all means speak with Coach Judi tomorrow. But take it from me; you have to learn to savor your victories in gymnastics—even when they're silver."

Nadia rolled her eyes. "Whatever you say, mother."

Nadia's mother gently lifted her daughter's chin so she could look into her eyes. "A gymnast's career is short," she said, her own eyes full of pain and regret. "Too short not to love every second of it."

And that's why YOU don't have a move named after you, Nadia thought. *But I will. Future generations of gymnasts will be watching my routines over and over again in their basements.*

TUMBLING DREAMS

You just wait and see.

CHAPTER 1: BACK TO WORK

Jamie linked arms with Kelley, her best Seattle friend and squad-mate. Together they skipped, Wizard of Oz-style, into their gym shout-singing Keshia's "Die Young."

Kelley's straggly brown hair had been plastered to her face by the rain, but Jamie's unruly black ringlets poofed up in defiance.

Kelley suddenly jerked them both to a stop.

"Oh my god!" she exclaimed. "I wish I could've been there to see you nail your floor routine! Did you really have the entire audience on their feet?"

"Well, not the entire audience," Jamie answered modestly.

"That's so hard to do to heavy metal," Kelley added.

"They would've been standing for you, too," Jamie said. "You should get Max to work that scoot and shuffle move from your dance recital into your floor choreography. It would give you such an edge."

It was a typical drizzly Seattle day with low-hanging clouds and minimal sun, but the girls didn't care. Jamie had just placed first all-around at Washington State's gymnastics competition and Kelley had finally convinced her mom to let her compete at Regionals with the rest of the girls on their squad—*if* the rules allowed it.

It was time for a victory dance.

"Race you to the door?" Kelley suggested.

"No fair!" cried Jamie. "You play soccer!"

"What's the matter?" teased Kelley. "Not fast enough?"

Kelley folded her arms into chicken wings and did the Funky Chicken in a circle around Jamie.

"Chiiiiiicken," she clucked.

Jamie narrowed her eyes in steely competition.

"On three," she stated. "One—"

"Two—" continued Kelley.

"Three!"

Both girls took off running toward the home of the Bellevue Kips. They slammed into the double glass doors at the same time and broke down into uncontrollable laughter.

Kelley managed to pull open the heavy doors and both girls fell into a happy but wet pile on a black-and-fuchsia sofa just inside the entryway. The entire gym was decorated in Kip colors—fuchsia, black, and silver. The squad loved it.

"Look what the cat dragged in," Nadia commented.

Jamie and Kelley exchanged a knowing look. Nadia was already in a mood.

"You're making a puddle," Nadia said before walking away to study up on the latest gymnastics news.

Jamie and Kelley broke down into another round of giggle fits.

"What's wrong with her?" Kelley asked. "I thought she placed second all-around."

"Yeah, but I placed first," Jamie stated matter-of-factly. She shrugged her shoulders, smiling.

Competing with your closest friends was all part of the deal in gymnastics.

In the locker room, Jamie and Kelley peeled off their wet jackets and rain boots and traded them for their team's black and fuchsia leotards.

Jamie checked herself out in the mirror. She kicked a strong straight leg up toward the ceiling.

She remembered standing tall at the top of the podium with her squad-mates Nadia and Bethany waving beside her. They'd placed first, second, and third, respectively.

Jamie had spent every day since dancing around singing.

Kelley stood beside her friend and tinkered with her ponytail in the mirror.

"Uh-oh," Kelley teased. "The victory is already going to your head. Wait, oh my god, is it actually getting bigger?"

"No," joked Jamie gently pushing Kelley aside. "It's just my hair getting bigger from all this rain. Does it ever stop?"

"Welcome to Seattle," Kelley said.

Jamie had only recently moved to the west coast from Miami with her mom. She missed the sun big time.

Kelley did a relevé onto her tippy toes as if she was also imagining herself on the podium.

"You are all so sooo lucky I wasn't at State to kick your butts," Kelley said. "You definitely would've been looking up at me."

A cloud passed over Jamie's eyes. She frowned for a second.

"Hey, Kelley," Jamie said in a more serious voice, tugging at a stray curl. "There's gonna be a lot of talk about State out there today. You gonna be upset you missed it?"

Kelley thought about it for a second.

"Maybe a little," she answered honestly. "I mean, I wish I could have been there competing with you guys, but my mom was right. I had a solo in my dance recital. I'd made a commitment. I couldn't let the other girls down."

Jamie scrutinized her friend's face in the mirror.

"And you're okay with your decision to cut back on dance and soccer so you can compete with us at Regionals?"

Kelley smiled cryptically. "Well, we'll see about that," she said.

The door opened, startling them.

Their squad-mate, Bethany, poked her blonde head through the door.

"When you two are done with your little slumber party," she began, "Judi wants to talk to us on the mats. Besides you can't leave me alone out there with Nadia. That girl is in the worst mood ever!"

Bethany let the door slap shut behind her, and Jamie and Kelley followed her to the gym floor. The Kips' gym was state-of-the art fancy and decorated in the team colors—fuchsia, silver, and black—right down to the crash mats.

Nadia, Bethany, and a group of younger recreational girls were already warming up to Flo Rida—an album Jamie had downloaded for Judi.

It still stunned Jamie to think of the contrast between her old gym and her new one. Everything in Bellevue was state-of-the-art fancy right down to the lemony-fresh scent. Her old gym smelled like a musty old basement because it kind of *was* a basement. Their crash mats were all hand-me-downs from the boys wrestling team.

Judi clapped her hands three times to get the girls' attention. Her freckled cheeks were rosy and her frizzy red hair had been wrangled into a single braid down her back. It was clear Judi was still riding the high from the State finals.

Jamie, Kelley, Bethany and Nadia clapped three times in response. It was super- lame preschool-style as far as everyone was concerned, but it worked every time.

"First of all," said Judi, "Congratulations on your performance at State. I think you all have something to be proud of." They all gave each other a round of applause and Nadia sat up extra-tall.

"Now," Judi said, changing her tone of voice. "Onto more serious topics. I'm sure you're all aware that Sara is not here and that she's had some problems staying focused lately."

A murmur of concerned and not-so-concerned chatter rippled through the group. Judi raised her eyebrows and they all quieted down.

"What you might not have realized is that Sara has been struggling with OCD," said Judi, "but I'm happy to report that she and her family are seeking help." Judi paused to let this information sink in.

"What's OCD?" asked Jamie.

"Obsessive compulsive disorder," Nadia informed her.

Bethany gasped. "Is that like...*contagious?*"

"No," said Judi. "It's behavioral. Sometimes people put a lot of pressure on themselves to succeed or be perfect and it's just not possible. They become afraid that something bad might happen and they invent rituals for themselves to help them feel calmer or more in control. Something reliable and predictable about, say, flicking on the light switch and watching the light go on. Does that make sense?"

"Oh my god!" exclaimed Jamie. "That's why she was braiding and unbraiding her hair all the time!"

Kelley nodded vigorously. "And zipping and unzipping her hoodie!" she added.

"Well, it's good that it's going to stop," said Bethany. "The sound was grating."

Kelley slapped her leg.

"What?" said Bethany. "It was." Bethany ran a finger through her long blond hair and let it fan out across her shoulders and down her back. Then she stretched her long body out on the mat and rested her head gently on the backs of her hands.

"It also explains all of the pre-event rituals she invented for herself," noted Judi.

"Like stepping on and off the mat three times before floor," Nadia clarified.

"Or clapping the chalk off her hands three times before bars," Kelley added.

"Poor Sara," said Jamie empathetically.

"Sara's doctors and parents are confident she'll make a full recovery," said Judi.

"Yeah, but will she do it in time for Regionals?" asked Bethany.

The rest of the squad glared at her, but they'd all been thinking the same thing.

You got such few chances in gymnastics. You were practically over the hill by the time you were seventeen.

You had to make every routine count.

And you had to make every competition a win.

CHAPTER 2: OCD

6:30 a.m.

Bethany dragged her exhausted body out of bed. She'd awoken in the middle of the night with throbbing pains in her shins, thighs and behind her knees. Even after rubbing Tiger Balm into her sore legs, she'd had a hard time falling back to sleep.

Growing pains, she thought. *Must be.*

A tragic soundtrack started playing inside her head as she steeled herself for the inevitable. "Back to Black" by Amy Winehouse, followed by some angry sounding P!NK.

She felt like Bella from Twilight going off to face the vampires.

Would Bethany have to sacrifice her love of gymnastics because she was born to a family of giants? Or even worse, would she start losing at comp because of her height?

The tragedy was already unfolding in Bethany's head. She quickly dressed herself, choosing a solemn gray-and-black fitted skirt and top as if she were going to a funeral. She painted her lips with a layer of sheer red lip gloss and pulled her long straight blond hair into a clean upsweep. If this was going to be her last day as a gymnast, she would receive the bad news in the appropriate attire.

Slowly, but with determination, she marched down the hall, like a medical patient walking into the doctor's office resigned to the fact that her test results would say, "TERMINAL".

"Good morning, Mother," she said dramatically as she walked into the kitchen.

Taking a slow deep breath, she watched her mother make coffee. Elenora Goddard was still beautiful for her age—elegant even. She'd always carried herself with confidence and pride even though she was freakishly tall.

Bethany scowled.

"Good morning, Bethany," said her mom, holding out a glass of fresh-squeezed orange juice.

Bethany grunted.

She headed straight for the doorpost where her siblings had been measuring their height since her oldest brother, now away at college, was a little kid. The ticks went up pretty high. The Goddards were a bunch of beanpoles.

Pressing her back against the wall, Bethany concentrated hard on compressing the space between each of her vertebrae.

"You know," said her mother, "most girls try to stand up as tall as possible when they're measuring themselves." She put down her coffee, walked over to Bethany and gently tucked her under the chin so she'd raise her head.

Bethany closed her eyes as if she were about to get a shot.

She felt her mom's fingers press against the back of her head.

"What does it say?" Bethany quickly asked. She sprung around to read the results on the wall, her eyes wide.

"Five feet, one quarter inches," her mom read aloud.

"That's a full eighth of an inch taller than last week!" Bethany's heart plummeted into her stomach on. She looked to her mother for sympathy.

Her mother frowned.

"Nature does as nature will, Bethany," her mother admonished. "All the measuring in the world is not going to change the fact that you come from a tall family."

"Oh, what do you know?!" Bethany burst out. "You like being an Amazon."

The word "brat" surfaced somewhere in the back of her mind, but she quickly shoved it away.

"You don't understand," she snapped. "You've never understood."

Bethany grabbed a granola bar off the table and stormed out the front door. She would pay for that move later. It always worked on TV, but somehow her mom never let it slide.

Right now she didn't care. She needed to make a statement. She needed—

--an umbrella.

"I hate you Seattle!" she cried out to the carpet of gray clouds hovering in the sky.

Bethany stormed back into the house and up the stairs for her umbrella.

"You know you're going to be grounded for that, don't you?" her mother asked as Bethany walked back out the door.

"Yes," Bethany said simply. "I do."

****

An entire school day of calculating math problems, debating persuasive arguments, and conjugating verbs in French did nothing to improve Bethany's mood. It all seemed so irrelevant to her future as a gymnast.

By the time she got to the gym, her body was pulsing with irritation.

She glared at her teammates. Kelley was linked with Jamie like a double-headed jolly monster and Nadia was listening to some floor routine music on her IPod while stretching.

Short people, she thought with contempt. *They don't know how lucky they are!*

She plopped herself down on a part of the mat as far away from her friends as possible.

Nadia rolled over onto her stomach and arched back into a stretch touching the back of her head to her toes.

"What's your problem?" Nadia asked pointedly.

Bethany imagined Nadia falling off the high bar because she was too short to jump up and grab it. She pulled off her own track pants and began her own warm-up ritual.

Sara was back. Predictably, Jamie and Kelley hovered around her bombarding her with chatter.

Great, thought Bethany, *something else to feel awkward about.*

"Okay, squad," said Judi, clapping her hands. "You know the drill. Run five laps and meet back here for stretching." Judi blew her whistle.

"Go!" she instructed.

Bethany ran around the gym, her legs bent slightly and her arms swinging at her sides. Running to prep for gymnastics was different than running in any other sport. In gymnastics competitions, running gave you the momentum to launch over the vault or propel yourself up to the high bar. The movements had to be purposeful and specific. And they made Bethany feel more purposeful with each stride. Last night's soreness had faded away.

Nadia was right—in a way.

If Bethany was on the verge of being too tall to compete, then every practice, every competition mattered. She would stand at the top of the podium at State championships. She would make them notice her. She would do better than third place.

Judi led the squad through a circuit at each apparatus, starting with the uneven bars. Jamie and Kelley quickly slipped on their grips, while Bethany and Nadia chalked up their hands—two tactics for reducing friction and preventing blisters.

This time, Sara was wearing grips, too. She'd torn her palms up before State finals when her skin became soft and dry from washing her hands too much—another one of her coping rituals. Grips braced your wrists *and* covered your palms. They'd help Sara protect the still-delicate skin on her hands.

Bethany and Nadia silently watched Sara tighten the straps. They were purists and they thought grips were wussy. They always teased Kelley and Jamie for using them, but somehow making fun of Sara seemed wrong.

Everyone was acting a bit awkward, even Jamie who was normally the master of any social situation.

"Why don't you go first, Sara?" Jamie offered, stepping off the mat.

Kelley backed away slightly as Sara passed.

Sara's eyebrows crinkled but she didn't say anything.

She jumped up onto the low bar and quickly lost her grip. She shook out her arms and legs.

"That's okay," said Jamie, "You'll get it next time."

"Yeah," Kelley was quick to jump in. "Grips take a while to get used to."

"I'm sure they do," said Sara, blowing her straight black bangs off her forehead.

Sara jumped back up and performed the beginning of her routine flawlessly, lifting her tiny body up on the low bar using the strength in her arms. Without hesitating, she swung herself around the bar until she'd built up enough momentum to flip to the high bar where she held her body in a handstand at the top of the movement.

But the weeks of inactivity made the first workout tough. Sara tried to work in one of the new compulsory elements—a bail/shoot from high to low bar—but she lost her grip and dropped to the floor landing on her feet.

"Nice try," said Jamie.

"Yeah, I'm sure you'll get it next time," Kelley added.

"NICE TRY?!" Sara snapped. "You'll get it next time? Argh! I just fell out of a transition! That's not how we talk to each other when we train. Where are the pointers? Where are the 'my mom can do a better bail/shoot than that's'?"

Sara let out a puff of air.

"I'm not sick," she said. "And I'm not crazy. Don't. Treat. Me. Differently. You're all making me feel like a freak!"

Silence.

Judi gave the girls a minute to work it out on their own.

"I'm sorry," said Jamie. "It's just that we don't know how to treat you."

"We don't want to be too critical," Kelley added.

Sara just stared at them. She turned to Nadia and Bethany, who seemed to be ignoring her.

"We—" Bethany started, but she ran out of words.

"I appreciate your concern," Sara told her squad-mates. "But please—my OCD is about *me.*" She struggled to find the right words. "*I* am the one who was putting too much pressure on me. Not you guys. The rituals—they just helped me feel more in control."

"In control of what?" Bethany asked.

"Life, stress, my schedule," Sara said. "The usual. All the things we always complain about." Sara took a breath.

"I'm learning healthier ways to take care of myself. In the meantime, can you please just treat me how you've always treated me?"

The girls were quiet, taking it all in.

"Well then," Nadia announced, breaking the tension. "You have to release the bar at the bottom of the swing or you'll never have enough momentum to do the layout with half turn. You're letting go too late. You need to tuck your butt in more during the extension or you'll never get enough height on that switch split. My mom can do better than that."

Sara smiled. "She probably still can."

Nadia's mom had competed at the Worlds Championships for Canada before retiring.

Jamie burst out laughing.

"Oh, Nadia!" she said. "Sometimes, I love you!"

CHAPTER 3: GROWING PAINS

"Do it," said Bethany squinching her eyes closed.

"No, don't do it!"

"NO, do it."

"No, don't."

Bethany and her mom stood in their kitchen doorway, Bethany's back pressed against the doorframe.

"Okay," Bethany closed her eyes. "I can't take it."

"Five feet one inch," her mother said flatly.

"NO!" Bethany wailed and sank to the ground.

"Three-quarters of an inch!" Bethany howled. "A whole three-quarters?! How is that even humanly possible? It's only been a week!"

Bethany was in the throes of a full-throttle freak-out.

This is tragic, she thought. *Tragic. I knew this day would come. I'm just too tall. Too tall for gymnastics. Gabrielle Douglas, Deng Linlin, Aliya Mustafina—all under five feet tall when they won Olympic gold.*

It's over, she thought. *My entire career. My hopes. My dreams. Everything. Drowned by the tick of a pencil against a doorpost.*

"One cartwheel will take from one end of the beam to the other." She looked up at her mom, her green eyes full of tears. "I'm going to cartwheel myself right off the end. Then I'll break my neck and be paralyzed and they'll make straight-to- DVD movies about my sad pathetic life, but no one will watch them—"

Tears were freely flowing from her eyes. She could tell her mother was trying really hard not to laugh and that made her even more angry and frantic.

Bethany felt like running back upstairs to bed, curling up under the covers, and staying there—*forever.*

"It's called a growth spurt," her mother offered calmly.

Bethany turned on her, but her mother met her with a warning glare. After the last outburst, she'd had all social media privileges taken away for a full four days. Bethany had felt like a giant freak banished to the depths of the forest to live out her sentence in isolation—cut-off from her entire social world.

This is why my center of gravity has been off in gym, she thought. Despite herself, she felt a little prick of relief. *At least there was a reason.* She shook her head. She let her mom wrap her arms around her.

Her mother took deep calming breaths until Bethany began imitating her.

"It is high time you cut through the drama and started gathering information," her mother said.

Bethany's mother led her by the shoulders to the computer and sat Bethany down in front of it.

Her mother typed, <<Olympic gymnasts height>> into the search engine and walked away.

Bethany went into a Google frenzy searching for facts about Olympic gymnasts. Nastia Liukin was the tallest gymnast in the 2008 U.S Olympic team at 5'3". She won Olympic gold in the all-around. The tallest was Svetlana Khorkina of Russia at 5'5". She was the first gymnast to win three all-around titles at the World Championships.

"Hmmm," Bethany said aloud. She wasn't sure what to think. Her shortest family member was her mom at a whopping 5' 11.

I'm only eleven and I'm already five-one, Bethany thought. *That means—*

The tears started flowing again.

Like a zombie, Bethany packed up her gear for gym and loaded herself into the car so her mother could drive her to the gym, a converted factory over on the outskirts of town.

At least the Kips will feel my pain, she thought. *Kelley will get it.*

But when she walked into the gym, her squad-mates were gathered around Jamie, and Kelley was giving her a bear hug.

"Jamie's grandmother is sick," Sara explained gently. "Her mom has to take off work to care for her."

Jamie struggled to find her breath between sobs.

"It's—it's—just," she gasped. Her eyes were red and puffy, but otherwise Jamie looked just as pretty when she was sobbing as she did when she was happy. "Money is already so tight. And gymnastics can be so expensive…and…and… *abuelita* means *everything* to me—"

"Don't worry," Nadia said. "Regionals are a full month away. We can help you out with the bus fare and maybe find you a scholarship for the competition fees."

"And you already have your uniform," Sara pointed out.

"And my mom can drive you to practices," Kelley offered.

Kelley gently stroked Jamie's hair.

She knew it was kind of petty, but Bethany felt like she'd been stabbed through the heart. Kelley was her best friend and she needed her.

First Jamie waltzes in and takes my spot on the podium, she thought. *Now when I need my friends most they're too busy consoling little-miss-perfect.*

"Well, if you have to take a couple of months off from gym because of money," said Bethany, "It's really no big deal. You can always babysit."

Jamie blinked her eyes a few times as if she couldn't quite understand what Bethany was saying.

Kelley shot Bethany a death glare and Bethany headed straight for the locker room to put on her leotard.

Nadia followed her.

"What's your problem?" Nadia began.

Not exactly consoling.

Bethany opened her mouth to answer, but she started crying instead.

Nadia looked panicked.

"Okay, then," she said, backing slowly toward the door. "When you're ready to talk, just—um, I guess, I'll be on beam."

Bethany nodded. Her shoulders heaved with sobs.

That's right, thought Bethany. *Run away. Go back to your precious Jamie. I'll handle this alone.*

APRIL ADAMS

CHAPTER 4: SERIOUS COMPETITION

Judi paced in front of a large dry-erase board, driving her point home.

Her curly reddish hair was being contained by what could only be called hair warfare bobby pins and hairpins and elastics and pincher clips everywhere. It wasn't doing a very good job. Seattle's rain had given Judi an intense case of the frizzies.

A ten-week intensive training schedule was posted on the board.

The gymnasts sat on the mats silently staring upward. Kelley twirled a strand of brown hair between her fingers.

Bethany rocked gently back and forth.

Jamie looked dazed.

Sara had to sit on her hands to keep from zipping her hoodie up and down.

Nadia was the only gymnast who didn't look visibly terrified.

"We have ten weeks until Regionals," Judi said emphatically.

Nadia tuned her out immediately. She'd heard it all before. She'd heard it that very morning from her mother, in fact. She knew the discipline and hard work the weeks ahead required of her and she was ready for them. This was casual dinner conversation at her house.

"That includes the disruptions of Thanksgiving and Christmas," Judi continued. "Basically, we don't have a lot of time."

"Since when do we ever have enough time?" Bethany muttered to Kelley.

The Regional competition would include four events: beam, bars, vault, and floor. For each event the girls would have to perform some required skills and combinations, called "compulsory skills" and some that were optional—or totally up to them and their coaches.

Judi and their choreographer, Max, had been careful to work a lot of these elements into their routines for the state finals so they'd only get better over time. But there were inevitably new skills to learn, new growth spurts to adjust to, and changes to the set of required skills.

"Compulsory and optional skills must be cleaned up before the competition," Judi went on. She looked at each of the girls in turn. "You all have room for improvement. And you are each strong in your own way."

"As you know, you have to be level 8 to compete at Regionals," Judi continued. "Since you all scored higher than a 31 during at least one competition this season, I'm bumping you all up. You've worked hard and you deserve it.

The girls all looked at one another, visibly relieved, except for Sara and Kelley.

"Finally, said Nadia. She bent sideways over her outstretched leg, elongated the muscles on her left side. Every waking moment was an opportunity for Nadia to stretch.

"Sara," said Judi, "You got a 31 at Optionals, so you are cleared to compete as well."

Sara avoided making eye contact but smiled. She zipped up the zipper on her hoodie, then realized she was only doing it because she was already nervous, and quickly stuffed her hands in her pockets.

"Great," she said, trying to sound properly enthusiastic.

Jamie reached over and grabbed her hand. Sara gave it a squeeze.

"Thank you," she mouthed.

Kelley squirmed in her seat.

As if reading her mind, Judi turned to Kelley.

"We're looking into making sure you can compete since you missed the State competitions," she said in a very business-like manner. "Your scores from Optionals certainly qualify you. In the meantime, you will train with everyone else as if you are definitely going to the competition."

Kelley smiled and nodded. It was something.

She really really *really* wanted to compete with her friends.

Jamie perked up and squeezed Kelley's knee.

"What that means on a practical level," Judi continued, "is that we'll have to add difficulty to all of your routines. The compulsory skills will be more difficult. And Max and I would like to choose some more complicated optional skills for you as well based on the strengths and weaknesses you showed during the last two competitions."

"Agreed?"

The girls nodded.

"The training schedule is posted here, in the locker room, and outside my office," Judi said. "Memorize it. Live by it." She caught herself sounding super intense and smiled.

"Eat it, drink it, sleep with it under your pillows," she joked.

"Kiss it goodnight before you go to sleep?" joked Jamie.

"Absolutely," agreed Judi. "Now, let's get to it. Run three laps and meet me at the uneven bars."

The only real difference between level 7 and level 8 on bars was that they now needed to have an element with flight or a 180-degree turn, like a pirouette out of a cast or a hiccup to the high bar. Sara and Nadia's routine already had that. And she and Kelley were both pros at casting to a perfect handstand on the high bar.

Kelley jumped up to perform the technique. She'd pulled a back muscle taking a throw-in during her last soccer game and her left shoulder was sore and tight. This move wasn't going to make it any better.

It was basic, but required a *ton* of shoulder strength. Kelley used the springboard to get up to the low bar. Facing the bar, she held herself up with her hips touching it. Then slowly *slowly* she pressed her legs up until she reached a handstand. Technically, even elite gymnasts were allowed to straddle their legs on the way up as long as they were pressed together during the handstand, but Kelley had always prided herself on her strength. No straddle for her.

"Excellent Kelley," called Judi. "Now do a pirouette, please."

Concentrating hard, Kelley let go with her right hand and turned her body, replacing her right hand to the far side of her left. She kept her legs long and tight.

Success!

Her shoulders strained with the effort.

"Excellent form, Kelley," said Judi. "That's enough for today. You may dismount."

Kelley swung her body around the bar and released, landing on the safety map with her feet together, knees slightly bent.

She smiled with relief and joy.

Shoulder pain aside, it felt so good to be working out again. She stretched one arm after the other across her chest.

"Take a minute to stretch out your arms and back, Kelley," called Judi. "We don't want you injured this early on in the season."

Gees, Kelley thought. *Judi* sees everything.

For the next four hours, the girls worked like crazy on the new compulsory components for each of their events.

Bethany and Jamie kicked butt on floor.

"Of course," said Kelley, "You're both drama queens!" Jamie gave her a playful swat, but Bethany pranced away to sulk.

"Takes one to know one," she responded.

Kelley and Nadia both excelled at beam. They were great at back walkovers and back handsprings and their routines already included flight, which was a fancy gym word for a jump. Sara, Bethany, and Jamie had a harder time searching out the bar with their feet.

Sara still struggled with backwards moves on all her events, but she was slowly gaining confidence. She'd broken both wrists doing a backflip on the beach last summer and the memories of the pain still freaked her out. Kelley wondered if that was maybe what had kicked off the OCD.

Bethany and Jamie struggled to find their balance on the new beam components, but all-in-all it wasn't a bad practice for their first intensive day back in the gym after competition.

"Okay, ladies," called Judi with her typical endless supply of enthusiasm. "Now that you're all warmed up, it's vault time."

"That was just the warm-up?" moaned Bethany. She was feeling sluggish and Judi's extra enthusiasm was putting her in a bad mood.

Judi clicked a button on a remote control and Lady Gaga blared through the gym's state-of-the-art sound system.

Jamie, Kelley, and Sara groaned while Bethany rolled her eyes.

"Sometimes you are such a dork," said Bethany.

"Respect for your elders, junior gymnast," Judi replied.

That actually got a smile out of Bethany, which was hard to do anywhere within ten feet of the vault. It was Bethany's most challenging event.

As the girls stretched out and Kelley wind-milled her arms to loosen up her shoulders, Judi explained that the vault had the biggest jump in difficulty between level 7 and level 8.

"At level 7, you only had to do a handspring," Judi noted.

"Only?" Bethany mumbled.

Judi ignored her sullen comments.

"If you want to be competitive at level 8, you'll need to complete a more advanced vault. And if you want the highest possible score, and I know you do," here, she paused to eye each of them in turn, "you'll need to do either a piked tsukahara or a yurchenko. Gymnastics moves were often named after the first gymnast to perform them. In this case, Mitsou Tsukahara and Natalia Yurchenko.

"What's a piked tsukahara?" asked Jamie.

"Nadia, would you care to demonstrate?" asked Judi.

"Of course," said Nadia as she walked proudly to the top of the runway.

God, Bethany muttered to Kelley. *She's never happier than when she knows more than everyone else does.*

Kelley ignored her friend. She loved watching Nadia vault. She was so strong, it was like watching someone being fired out of a cannon.

Nadia ran, jumped, touched the bar with both hands, and did a series of flips. It all happened so quickly, Jamie could hardly make out the individual moves.

"The tsukahara is named after Japanese five-time Olympic gold-medalist, Mitsou Tsukahara. He's also known for his full-twisting double salto in the tuck position," said Nadia. "He last competed in 1978."

"Show-off," muttered Bethany. She stood off to the side of the group with her arms crossed, pouting.

"Thank you Nadia," said Judi.

27

"Now, I'm going to ask Nadia to do that again and I want you all to focus on how she jumps off the springboard and performs a quarter turn onto the horse," said Judi. "Then she'll push off with her hands into a back flip, and because it's piked, one or more pikes into the dismount."

Jamie watched as Nadia started her run with one foot and one arm extended out in front of her like a dancer. She pumped her arms as she ran toward the horse to build momentum for the vault.

As she jumped up off the springboard she turned her body into what looked like a sideways handstand placing both hands on the horse, her legs together, and then quickly bent her body in half at the waist with her arms and legs straight and flipped forward in the air twice—the two pikes.

It was awesome.

"Whoa," said Jamie, applauding. "Can you do that again?"

"You'll all have a chance," said Judi. "Why don't you give it a try, Jamie? Remember to push down on the vault with both hands to get enough height for the turns."

Jamie took her position at the top of the mat.

I can do this, she thought, but she didn't feel as focused as usual. Her grandma was still in the hospital and Jamie walked around with a constant knot of worry in her stomach.

She managed a handstand on the horse into a flailing crash landing. Kelley was up next and got it almost right but with fewer rotations.

"We are going to be sore tomorrow," Kelley joked rubbing her throbbing shoulders.

"Tell me about it," said Jamie. "I think mine was more of a fluke than a Tsuk."

Kelley groaned at the forced rhyme.

Jamie was trying hard to maintain a good sense of humor, but every time she quieted her mind, she saw an image of her grandmother collapsed on the kitchen floor and a dagger of pain jabbed her in the stomach.

"We'll save the Yurchenko for tomorrow," Judi said. "I know most of you have already done one of these for State anyway. One skill at a time. Bethany, you're up."

Bethany nodded and took her place at the top of the runway as if the vault were no big deal—as if she hadn't crashed into it during what felt like a million practices before Optionals and State.

She took a deep breath, saluted the imaginary judges, and ran toward the horse. She bounced on the springboard and managed to maintain a handstand before crashing onto the mats.

She landed right on her hipbone.

"Ugh!" Bethany exploded. "This is impossible! I'm just too tall for this!"

"You just need to get more height when you push off the horse," said Sara. "It'll help you get all your rotations in."

"It'll help you get all your rotations in," mimicked Bethany. "Since when are *you* the expert? You didn't even medal."

The rest of the squad snapped to attention.

"Bethany, that is enough" Judi commanded. "I will not have you insulting your fellow gymnasts. We are a team. Your height has nothing to do with your difficulties on vault. We have been over this."

To prove her point, Judi ran with her lean, 5' 5' adult body toward the horse, bounced up, pushed over, and twisted over with strength and ease.

Seven seconds later she stood at the other end, her cheeks rosy and her breath short from the effort.

"Were you watching?" she asked. "Did you see the way I tucked my ribs into my abdominals? That's what you need to do on vault. It's about core strength and focus. Not body length. You are so busy fretting about your height at the beginning of the mat that you are not focusing on the key aspects of vault—which all happen in preflight and have absolutely nothing to do with how tall you are."

Judi was stern, but not angry. Kelley wondered what it would take for Judi to completely lose her patience with Bethany.

"You have to push down to jump up," Kelley offered. "Just like you do in your floor routine."

"Or the way that you push down on the bar to lift up into a kip," suggested Nadia. "It's no different."

Bethany glared at her friends' unwelcome advice.

"In fact," said Judi, looking a bit drained. "Why don't you all work on core strength before you head home."

The girls groaned.

"Nadia, please lead the stomach crunches," she instructed. "One hundred on each muscle group. I'll be in my office. Happy Thanksgiving. I expect you all to come back with renewed focus."

"What's her problem?" Bethany grumbled.

"You," said Nadia.

"Thanks a lot, Bethany," added Kelley. "You broke Judi."

Sara rolled her eyes.

Nadia didn't waste time getting her teammates onto the mats for crunches. She didn't mind the extra work. She was willing to do whatever it took to succeed.

And, unlike her squad-mates, *she* was willing to do it without the drama.

CHAPTER 5: GIVING THANKS

"Mami!" Jamie called as she mashed the potatoes for Thanksgiving dinner.

Jamie peered into the oven at the turkey.

"Is it supposed to look like that?" she asked her mom. The legs were super brown, but the rest of the skin was still a pale golden color.

"And shouldn't the marshmallows on top of the sweet potatoes be more...*melty?"* she asked.

"Well, we're not going to get invited onto Iron Chef," her mom joked, "but I don't think we're that far off."

"It looks sickly," Jamie half-joked. "Maybe we should have deep-fried it. Her lower lip momentarily popped out in a pout. Jamie was used to spending Thanksgiving in Miami in a mass of family and friends. Her *abuela* and a few stray cousins always flew down to join them. The day after, they all made turkey sandwiches or *arroz con pavo* out of the leftovers and headed to the beach for a lazy picnic.

Abuela had always been the *jefa* in charge of the turkey.

This year, she was too weak and sick to join them in the kitchen.

This year, they got a recipe for a smaller bird off some website. Turkey for three definitely looked a bit...skimpy.

"Mmmmm," her mom looked at the goopy mess of sweet potatoes and molten marshmallows. "I don't know," she said. "Your *abuela* always makes them."

"I'll go show her," Jamie suggested.

Jamie blew a stray strand of frizzy black hair off her forehead with a puff of air. This Seattle weather was getting old.

Everything was always wet—and cold. Who knew an umbrella cover in a shopping mall was standard Seattle-area protocol? Who knew they even existed?

Jamie pulled on two giant-sized oven mitts and carried the under-sized Turkey for three into her grandmother's bedroom

Bzzz, her cellphone buzzed in her pocket. Her Miami friends and cousins had been texting all day to wish her a happy Thanksgiving or to let her know how sad they were that she couldn't be there to celebrate with them this year.

It made her feel appreciated but sad at the same time. She was grateful for the love, but she hated missing out.

"Abuelita," Jamie said gently as she entered her grandmother's bedroom.

Jamie was assaulted by the medicinal smells of hospital as soon as she opened the door. Could a bed bring that with it or was it just the smell of sick?

Her grandma was raised up on a hospital bed they'd rented to make her more comfortable watching the Macy's parade on TV.

"Ooh, a Glee float!" said Jamie, trying to squelch her sadness.

Her grandmother slowly turned her head and struggled to smile.

"Mi cielito," she said. My heaven.

"Abuela," Jamie continued, she brought the turkey bedside. "We can't tell if the turkey---

Her grandmother's body was suddenly wracked by retching sounds and she grabbed for the plastic basin beside her. The smell of the turkey was just too strong. It had made her nauseous.

Jamie raced to put the turkey in the hallway. She knelt beside the bed and lifted a cup of room temperature ginger ale to her grandmother's lips.

Her mom rushed in behind her.

Jamie silently wept as her mother helped her grandmother.

I'm thankful you're still with us, Jamie thought, *leaning her head against her grandmother's bed.*

I'm so so thankful.

The twin tornadoes, who were Sara's younger brothers, blew in and out of the dining room leaving a mess of silverware next to a bunch of plates on the dining room table.

Spaceship noises marked their exit.

Miraculously, most of the utensils were in the right places. Their parents had trained them well.

Sarah tidied up the silverware beside each plate, from salad fork to dinner fork. Each one was perfectly parallel, just like her mother had taught her.

Sara's older sister, Yeji, stopped setting out the glasses to watch her little sister. Yeji had been named after their dad's mom on the Japanese side of the family while Sara had been named after her mom's mom. Leaning across the table, Yeji shifted one of the forks so that it jutted away from the plate at an angle.

Sara caught her eye and her sister's face gleamed with mischief. Catching on, Sara flicked a butter knife so that it messed up the neat placement of all the other silverware.

She giggled.

Sara's mother pulled a steaming hot plate of roasted Brussels sprouts out of the oven and watched her girls.

With one eyebrow raised she walked over to the table.

Sara and her sister caught their breath.

"This year, I'm grateful for the small victories," Sara's mother said, "and shifting family priorities." With an uncharacteristic giggle, she knocked over an empty glass. Then she burst into full-on laughter.

It was contagious.

"Me, too," said Sara, "Like sleeping through the night without waking up to check the alarm clock setting twenty times."

"Oh, did you make it through the night last night?" Sara's sister joked.

Sara bunched up a napkin and threw a napkin at her.

She held up an empty glass for a toast.

"Here's to leaving the house without locking the door three times!" she said.

Their mother picked up another glass. "To washing our hands once and only when they're dirty."

Sara laughed, a happy-bitter laugh. That one was still tough.

"To a more realistic standard of excellence," she said.

The three Sato's chinked glasses.

"And to not freaking out because toasting with empty glasses is supposedly bad luck," Sara's sister joked.

"It is?" Sara felt a momentary surge of panic.

Sara's mom placed a soothing hand on Sara's silky black hair.

"It's toasting with water that is bad luck," she said, "and only in certain cultures. Toasting, itself, started with the ancient Greeks who had an interesting habit of spiking the punch with poison. Offering a toast was deemed a gesture of good faith. The term toasting comes from the Roman practice of—"

"Mooooom!" Sara howled. "It's a holiday!"

Her sister rolled her eyes.

She swatted her mom with a rolled up cloth napkin and they all devolved into laughter once again.

"What?" said her mother. "Just because we're developing more realistic standards, doesn't mean I'm going to let a teachable moment pass by unnoticed."

****

Bethany usually loved Thanksgiving, but this year she resented the disruption in her training schedule. She only had a few weeks to go from third place all-around to first, and it was bad enough she had an extra three-quarters of an inch to deal with—she didn't need an over-indulgent holiday adding extra pounds.

Bethany placed a long piece of string out on her rec room floor, pretending it was a balance beam, and slowly moved through her routine.

The sounds of football and the smells of slow-roasting turkey and stuffing filled the house. Within an hour, her house would be full of abnormally tall aunts, uncles, cousins and even a grandpa who hadn't seemed to shrink at all over the years.

Giants, Bethany thought.

WHACK! A pillow hit her dead in the head.

"Yo, beanpole," called her brother from the sofa, "Your gargantuan cranium is blocking the TV!"

"I am not a beanpole and at least I didn't spend the day trying to snack my way into morbid obesity like you," Bethany snipped. It was bad enough she'd have to work off all the calories they were about to consume, but her brothers wouldn't even let her practice in peace.

"I'll have your portion, beanpole," her other brother agreed. Having them home from college was fun, but she hadn't realized how used to *not* having them around she'd gotten.

Bethany's mom came halfway down the stairs and looked over the railing.

"Bethany, can I talk to you for a second, please?"

Sure, Bethany thought, *they're being selfish and I'm the one getting in trouble.*

"Uh-oh, beanpole's in trouble," her brothers teased.

"I've noticed you've been in a little bit of a funk lately," her mom began.

Bethany clicked her tongue and huffed, but before she could blow her top, her mom handed her a small red handmade book.

Bethany looked from the book to her mom confused.

Her mom smiled proudly.

"I thought this might help make you feel better," her mom said. "Open it."

Bethany lifted up the red cloth cover. The book was a smaller version of the notebook Bethany kept with pasted images of favorite routines and moves—kind of like a tangible version of a Pinterest board.

Handwritten at the top of the first page in her mother's careful script were the words, "Things I am Thankful to Know."

Bethany turned the page. Each one featured one of twenty gymnasts over 5'7" who went on to successful careers in gymnastics and in other fields. Her mom had humorously drawn a tape measure next to each one.

Bethany's eyes filled with tears.

"Keep flipping," her mom encouraged, like a proud six-year-old who'd just cooked breakfast in bed for her parents.

"Top Model Salaries for 2012?"

Each of these beautiful women also had a tape measure drawn next to their catwalk poses. Not a single one was under 5'11.

Bethany felt a heavy weight lifting off her chest.

She kept turning the pages.

"Top Performance Careers for Gymnasts"

Pages of images of Cirque du Soleil, dance performances, and rhythmic gymnastics had been carefully glued inside in the book.

Bethany hugged her mom.

"You're the best," she said.

Her mom squeezed her tightly. Bethany's head nestled on her mom's shoulder and her mom kissed the top of it.

"Still short enough to do that," she said.

"Thank you," said Bethany. "Thank you so very much."

****

Kelley's family sat at a dining room table full of steaming plates of turkey, broccoli, mashed potatoes, sweet potatoes, and stuffing.

Her stomach rumbled. She'd gone for a long run that morning and she was famished.

The pile of hot string beans drizzled with honey, lemon, and walnuts sitting on the table beside her was not helping.

Her soccer team had done a Turkey Trot that morning—a 5K race above Golden Gardens Park.

They'd worn their green and gold Falcons uniforms and passed a soccer ball around the whole way, like a big extended family. Kelley still felt the warm glow of friendship.

She also felt faint. She needed to get some food in her belly—and fast! But first her family had to go around the table and say what they were each thankful for in *one word*.

"Family," her dad began.

"Friends."

"Maroon 5."

"Star Wars."

Kelley tried to focus on being grateful, but the wafting smell of melted butter on garlic bread whittled its way into her consciousness.

Kelley thought she would be grateful if her stomach didn't digest itself. But really she was thankful for her gym squad, her dance troop, *and* her soccer team.

Was there just one word for all of that?

"Seattle's low crime rate," said her aunt.

"Uncle Peter's successful hernia operation," said her great-aunt.

"My talented children," said her mom next to her as she squeezed Kelley's hand.

Kelley was up.

"I'm thankful for…" All at once she felt everyone's attention focused on her and panicked a bit.

"Fitness," she finally said, summing it all up.

Her father gave her a quizzical look and then smiled.

"Lovely," he said. "Now let's eat!"

CHAPTER 6: VAULTING FEARS

"Grrrrr." Bethany was splayed out on the mat clutching her stomach. She forced herself to roll over.

"Why? *Why?!*" she wailed. "Why do I do it to myself every year?" She felt like someone had sewn a dumbbell into the lining of her leotard.

"Too. Much. Pie," she said dramatically, as if she were on her deathbed.

Jamie laughed.

"Our pie was store-bought and gross," she said. "I should be faster than everyone." She pushed herself up and onto her feet. It was time for laps. "Except I made up for it by eating second dinner," she whispered to Kelley.

"I love second dinner!" added Sara. "It's just not Thanksgiving without the feeling that your stomach may explode at any moment."

"If I have to resist Eastern European grandmother trying to force feed me potato kugelis," Nadia began, "you can all resist your own hands lifting the fork to your mouths."

"Nope, nope," said Bethany shaking out her blond locks. "Can't do it. Science. Science says it's impossible."

"Resist the force you cannot," said Kelley in a Yoda voice.

"You're different, Nadia," said Sara. "I bet your mom stuck to your training schedule through the holiday."

Kelley laughed. "You probably have a balance beam in your

basement."

Nadia looked away.

Bethany chuckled. "Does your mom dangle a piece of turkey at the end of the beam and make you back handspring for it?"

"That is not as far off as you may think," said Nadia, as she took off running.

The rest of the squad reluctantly followed her.

Max had come in today to help them fine-tune their floor routines. If Kelley had to say what made her grateful for Max in a single word, it would be "awesome." He was awesome at picking their songs, awesome at playing to their strengths, and awesome at putting together dynamic routines that got the crowd excited.

One-by-one, he called them over to mat. Floor routines lasted a total of 90 seconds and included both acrobatic and dance moves, so a gymnast could really play to her strengths. It was also the only event set to music—not that Max and Judi let the gymnasts choose their own soundtracks.

The compulsory elements for level 8 floor were: a tumbling pass with two saltos; three different kinds of salto within the routine; a leap or jump with a 180° split; and the last tumbling pass also had to include a salto. There would be a half-point deduction for each missing special requirement.

No biggie for most of them. Just a few extra flips or rolls mainly.

Kelley bounced over to the mat. She missed dancing. She'd had to scale back on her extra-curricular activities and only got to go to dance workshops once in a while. Floor was now the closest she got to performing. Except today, they were mostly working on the acrobatic elements.

Kelley pressed down on the floor mat with her feet in order to jump up into a split. It was a little harder to get all the way to 180 degrees since she'd cut-out dance. She just didn't feel as flexible—especially since she'd kept up with soccer, which had nothing to do with stretching and elongating muscles.

"What happened to your split," teased Max. "Too much turkey?"

Kelley felt so frustrated tears welled up in her eyes. If she did dance, she didn't have enough time for gym, but without dance, her gym wasn't as good. She felt trapped in a twisted cycle.

How does anyone else make it work?

"Hey, Teary-Eyes," noted Sara, "What's up?"

"Just feeling a little more sore and a lot less flexible than I did when I was dancing."

"Ah," said Sara, "That sounds hard."

"Yeah," said Kelley.

Sara awkwardly placed a consoling hand on Kelley's back. She understood how it felt to have to make sacrifices. As a rule, she wasn't a super touchy person, but she didn't know what else to do or say.

She felt Kelley's pain. You needed to do it all to be good, but you couldn't possibly do it all. Sometimes, she thought it was amazing that anyone succeeded at this sport.

Sara took her position next to Max and Kelley used the opportunity to get in some extra stretching and practice on dance moves. Kelley noticed that Max had incorporated a few dance steps into Sara's routine that imitated a few of her rituals—like taking three steps forward and three steps back. Kelley wasn't sure it was exactly in keeping with Sara's therapy, but she liked Max's style.

Afterwards, Bethany worked with Max on incorporating a wider variety of saltos into her routine.

"Oh, my goodness, Bethany," Kelley squealed. "We learned this move in dance a couple of weeks ago that would be perfect in your routine—right before you do your last tumbling pass."

"A couple of weeks ago?" Bethany asked, an eyebrow arched. "Not last night?"

"Har har," Kelley said sarcastically. She fought to hold back the tears again. Sometimes Bethany's jokes weren't exactly friendly.

"Argh, Bethany!" Sara cried to break the tension. "I just gave her a whole pep talk about that!"

"Okay, okay, sorry," Bethany said. "Didn't realize you were so *sensitive*. Come teach me this move of yours."

Kelley brightened up and demonstrated a complicated series of sweeps and sashays. Bethany liked the fluid way Kelley moved. She imagined herself dancing on a stage. She imagined an audience applauding her every gesture.

"Ooh, I like it," Bethany cooed. "Very Lady Gaga."

"Me too," said Max. "It's very stylized. It's in."

Meanwhile, Judi worked with the rest of the squad on their compulsory vault. Nadia, Kelley, and Sara all had it almost set and were working on minor tweaks.

"Nice height, Sara!" called Kelley.

"Are you only saying that because—" Sara started.

"No," said Nadia. "She's saying it because you got great height."

"Good work, ladies," said Judi.

Bethany finished up on floor work with Max and ran over to join Jamie, the only other Kip who was still struggling.

"I don't get it!" exclaimed Jamie, more frustrated than usual. "What is everyone else doing that I'm not?"

"The vault," said Bethany.

"I can't get a full rotation in for the pike," said Jamie. "It doesn't make any sense. I can do a yurchenko and that's like, almost the same thing. Is it my core? Do I need to do more stomach crunches? What's the deal?"

Soon her friends were commiserating with her.

"Remember when you couldn't stick your landings on beam before Optionals?" asked Sara. "You worked it and worked it and worked it until you got it. That's all it takes. Hard work. Practice."

Jamie laughed. "You sound like my mom."

Bethany separated herself from the group to sulk.

Of course, they're all helping Jamie, she thought bitterly. *Precious delicate, Jamie.*

After vault, they moved onto beam, which was off for everyone.

"How can we balance?!" Jamie lamented. "I have a whole extra five pounds of turkey to adjust to!"

Kelley made gobbly turkey noises and chased Jamie around the beam. The rest of the girls backed out of the way.

"Hey, Nadia," called Sara. "Your mom's here."

Nadia's mother had been watching them all struggle from the parents' lounge. She often came to watch practices, but she rarely allowed herself to step out onto the floor.

"Oh, I know," said Nadia. "I have to go to the dentist after practice today.

"Hello girls," said Mrs. Hodvic . "I see you're all having a hard time with beam today."

"Mother, this is not the time," said Nadia.

"Oh, you hush," said Nadia's mother. She was a short woman who still had the broad shoulders and big smile of a gymnast. Her posture was so perfect, she made Nadia look like she was slouching. She was still in great gym shape.

"I'm not here to criticize," she said. "I was just reminded of the time before my squad's Nationals competition. I was at level 9 or 10, I think. We'd been struggling with beam all day…"

"What helped?" asked Sara.

"What I can tell you is that most problems in gymnastics are all about the basics. All the fancy stuff builds off a strong foundation. Can't get a vault? Maybe it's your running. Can't stick to the beam? Maybe you need to practice balance."

Sara nodded, but Nadia just rolled her eyes as if she'd heard it all before.

"Okay, but what did you do?" asked Bethany. Nadia's squad-mates were eager for any tips they could get. Nadia's mother was a former world champion. It was not every day they got to pick her brain.

"We worked really hard on our foundationals—core strength, running, upper body strength. If we gossiped, we did it in the plank position. And then, we had a piñata party."

"A what?" Jamie asked.

"We had a slumber party and smashed a piñata," said Nadia's mom. "If you can hit a moving object with your eyes closed, your feet can find the beam. Let's just say, we were all standing on the podium later that month—plus it feels good to smash something."

Nadia's mom smiled at them.

"Our basement is always available whenever you girls are ready to have a slumber party," she added, before jingling her car keys, her signal to Nadia that it was time to stretch out and get ready to go.

Nadia was infused with intense pride for her mother and all of her accomplishments. Her mother had set boundaries—strong ones—but she was balanced and she'd taught Nadia well.

Nadia didn't know if she could succeed without her mother by her side. And for the first time, she felt like she could stop competing with her mother's legacy.

"Mom," she said, as they walked toward the parking lot. "Thank you."

CHAPTER 7: SECRETS

Kelley cracked open the locker room door and poked her head out. She looked left. She looked right.

All clear.

Slowly, she inched her body out of the locker room. A zebra print rain slicker hid her gold-and-green Falcon's jersey. She'd promised her mom and herself that she'd cut back on her other activities to focus on gym, but her team had a big game against the Ducks today. They needed her killer corner kick.

Besides, she nailed the compulsory vault yesterday. No one would even miss her. She held an ice pack against her shoulders just in case— her built-in excuse.

"She's not getting it."

"Neither is Jamie."

Kelley stopped short.

That was Judi's serious voice. Max's, too.

Kelley peeked her head around the corner and saw Bethany run toward the horse, pumping her arms. At the springboard, she bounced up into the air. She touched the horse with two hands, but she couldn't get her legs to follow her.

She ended up doing a super-ungraceful handstand and fell to the mat, landing on her butt.

"Arrrgh!" she cried in frustration. Nearby, Nadia was giving Jamie pointers on the same vault.

At least Bethany's not alone, thought Kelley, as she tiptoed toward the door. *She can't blame it on her height if Jamie is struggling, too.*

"What do you want to do?" That was Max, their choreographer. Lately, he'd been assuming the role of assistant coach more and more.

"I don't know," said Judi. Her voice sounded tired, frustrated—a lot like Sara's when she couldn't get a skill down. "We don't have much time."

Kelley's heart pounded. Judi and Max were facing the vault, watching Jamie fall on her dismount—again.

"Bump them down a level?" asked Max.

"Can't," answered Judi. "Level 8 is the minimum for Regionals. The squad will never medal in the team all-around unless everyone completes a vault with a high start value."

"Take them out of the competition?" Max suggested. "Send them to a Level 7 optional event instead? We have Kelley as backup."

"That may be the kindest solution," answered Judi. "But it's one I'd prefer to avoid."

Kelley leaned back against the wall feeling panicked and guilty. This was not good.

I should tell Jamie and Bethany, she thought. *No, they'd flip. Bethany for sure would throw a temper tantrum, and Jamie's got enough to worry about with her grandma.*

But I can't keep this to myself, she reasoned. *Tell Sara? No. It would totally stress her out.*

Nadia? Not a chance. She'd hold it against them as a weakness. Things are tense enough.

I hate secrets! Kelley thought.

Just then, Kelley heard applause and cheering. She peeked her head back around the corner to see Bethany standing tall and triumphant on the other side of the horse. Jamie ran over and hugged her.

"Now you have to teach me!" Jamie cried.

Kelley giggled with relief. *One down,* she thought. *One to go.*

Time check. Fifteen minutes to soccer. Kelley would have to run.

She bolted toward the door and collided with Sara, who was holding a bloody rag up to her top lip.

Kelley stared at it in horror.

"Please don't tell!" whispered Sara, her eyes were wide.

"Tell what?" asked Kelley. She pulled Sara's hand away from her mouth. Her top lip looked like she'd been biting it until it bled.

"I just get so scared that I'm going to mess up and fall and get hurt," said Sara. "It's like I don't even feel it until it's bleeding." Sara's eyes were pleading.

Kelley locked eyes with Sara. There was so much hurt and Kelley couldn't do anything to help her.

She put a hand on Sara's shoulder.

This was an afternoon of big complicated decisions and Kelley didn't feel up to the task. Her own stomach felt like a swarm of bees were racing around inside it Motocross-style. She forced herself not to do another time check.

What's more loyal? Kelley thought, *keeping a friend's secret or saying something to someone who could help her?*

Sara glanced at Kelley's green bag. Everyone in the gym knew Kelley color-coded her gear so she'd never show up for a game or practice with cleats instead of ballet slippers.

"Does your mom know you're playing?" Sara asked.

It was a simple question, not a threat, but it was a question that clearly said, "We're in the same boat."

Kelley felt caught.

Just then the girls heard a screech like someone had stepped on a cat's tail.

They snapped their heads toward the floor in time to see Judi and Max running over to the beam.

Nadia sat on the floor beside the beam, grabbing her ankle and rocking back and forth.

"What were you doing on beam without a spotter?!" Judi cried.

That's my cue, Kelley thought.

"Gotta run", she said to Sara. "Text me if Nadia's ok." She handed her friend one of her ice packs.

"I'm not saying anything," she whispered. "But ice that lip and stop chewing on it or I will."

With that, Kelley turned and bolted out the door.

CHAPTER 8: FRACTURED FRIENDSHIPS

The mood at the gym the next day was solemn.

No laughing, no joking, no chatting. There was barely even any smiling.

Jamie's eyes were swollen and puffy as if she'd spend the night awake and crying. She forced herself to smile when Kelley came in to say hello, but then took off to run laps.

Bethany was wired—both happy she'd *finally* nailed the vault the day before and stressed that she might not be able to do it again.

It seemed only Nadia was chill. She calmly taped up her ankle for the day's workout.

"Just twisted," she said when she caught Kelley watching her. "But thanks for asking."

Whatever, thought Kelley.

She moved over to the mat to pull off her own sweatpants and get ready for practice.

"Nadia's mom probably has an electromagnetic massage machine for just such an emergency," Bethany muttered.

"Like a backup generator during a blackout?" Kelley joked.

"Precisely."

Kelley had shown up early for today's practice to make up for leaving early the day before. Still, she couldn't shake the dreads. If anyone asked where she'd been, she'd have to tell the truth but she wasn't sure she could handle the consequences.

Luckily, no one was paying attention to her.

Judi was too distracted by the Sara situation to call Kelley out on sneaking off.

Sara had shown up with her lip swollen and torn. The rest of the gymnasts couldn't help but stare and whisper about it.

Uncomfortable with the negative attention, Sara took off running a good twenty yards behind Jamie.

Our team is going to end up being in super-shape if all this tension keeps up, thought Kelley.

Bethany interrupted her thoughts.

"Ick," she said, clearly disgusted. "How could anyone do that to themselves? I just don't get it."

"Well, we're all having a hard time dealing with the pressure," said Kelley. "How do *you* handle stress?"

"I stress out!" shouted Bethany. "That's how I handle stress. I don't hurt myself."

No, you just hurt everyone else, Kelley thought. Lately she'd felt the divide between her and Bethany growing wider and wider. Bethany resented both Kelley's age (she was one year younger) and height. Those were not things Kelley could do anything about. Even her friendship with Jamie seemed to annoy Bethany. Kelley just didn't get it.

"And don't think I didn't notice you sneaking off to soccer yesterday," Bethany added. "You had GUILT scrawled across your whole face. Way to support me when I was struggling with vault."

"What?!" Kelley opened her mouth, speechless.

Her point made, Bethany marched over to the mat and stretched out beside Nadia as if making some sort of dramatic statement.

Kelley stretched out her sore shoulders. Soccer had felt like a welcome break from the physical stress of handsprings, handstands, front walkovers, and a million-and-one other moves that required upper-body strength.

It had also been a chance to work together as a team instead of bickering like a bunch of warring factions.

"Nadia," said Judi, "Has your mom cleared you to train?"

"Yes," said Nadia. She handed Judi a note. She was careful not to limp. Judi would be looking for any signs of pain or discomfort.

"Good," she said. "I want you to take it easy today. No jumps. Just walk your way through the routines. Tomorrow you can participate full-on."

Nadia's nostrils flared briefly, but she kept her composure.

"Of course," she replied through gritted teeth. Nadia pulled out her iPod and put the ear buds in, most likely listening to the commentary on some world-champion gymnast's floor routine as she stretched out.

Half-an-hour later, Judi had them back on vault. Kelley completed a full Tsuk on her second attempt.

Yay! she thought, newly confident that sneaking off to soccer had been the healthy thing to do.

Sara had decided to deal with the stares and looks of concern or contempt by pretending everyone else was not there. In a strange way, it helped her concentration.

She made it over the horse in the perfect pike position and managed to get in two rotations before she landed. She raised her arms up above her head and smiled briefly before her face contorted in pain.

Bethany did one almost-right vault and then fumbled the second.

"I had it yesterday!" she whined.

"Okay, beam is next," Judi announced. "Kelley, how are your shoulders?"

"Eh," Kelley said.

"Okay, let's see," said Judi.

Kelley had done a shoulder mount on beam for Optionals earlier in the fall. That was going to be rough with her injury. She tried to be tough like Nadia as she sprang up from the board onto the beam, but she couldn't hide a grimace of pain. Within two seconds, she flailed to the crash mat below her.

Judi sighed. Her whole team was struggling. She sat down on the mat beside Kelley and helped her get an extra stretch in her shoulders.

She didn't say anything for a full minute. The girls watched her silently, not sure what to expect. Eventually Judi looked up at her squad, resigned.

"Who wants to go on a field trip?" she asked.

Jamie's eyes lit up.

Sara and Nadia were confused.

"Is this a trick?" Bethany asked.

"No," said Judi plainly as she stood up. "My hard workers need a break."

Jamie and Kelley made eye contact across the floor. Kelley wiggled her eyebrows.

"I'd go on a field trip," Kelley offered.

"Good," said Judi. "Then it's decided. All of you put on your track suits and running shoes and meet back here in five minutes."

"I knew this was a trick," Bethany groaned.

Five minutes later the girls were headed out of the gym and into the late-autumn drizzle. They jogged toward the center of town with Judi in the lead and Sara lagging about twenty feet behind.

Nadia and Bethany ran side-by-side

"I thought I was supposed to take it easy on my ankle," Nadia complained.

"Some field trip," Bethany whined.

"I *hate* running," Jamie confided to Kelley. "How do you do this all the time? It's so *boring.*"

"It's easier when I'm chasing a ball," Kelley admitted.

"How much further?" Bethany asked just quietly enough that Judi wouldn't hear her.

Judi led them along the sidewalk and down two backstreets. The traffic was fairly quiet for a weekday afternoon.

They rounded a corner and the mall loomed up ahead of them.

"We're going shopping!" Bethany squealed. Her face lit up with excitement.

"There's no *shopping* in gymnastics," Nadia stated.

Judi didn't wait for more reactions. She jogged toward the mall at a brisk pace and the girls were forced to follow. When they got inside, she stopped them in front of Qoola and smiled.

"Frozen yogurt on me!" she declared. "And no skimping on toppings!"

"Oh my god, Judi, you're the best coach *ever!*" Jamie exclaimed, stopping just short of hugging her. "I love Qoola!"

Judi shrugged. "I know."

The girls picked their flavors and toppings and walked back to the gym at a leisurely pace savoring each bite.

Nadia and Bethany led the way, talking strategy. Sara allowed herself to join the group and chatted happily with Jamie and Kelley. The cool frozen yogurt soothed her sore lip.

"Did you guys *see* the boy behind the counter?" Jamie asked.

"The one with the shaved hair and nose ring?" Sara asked.

"NO!" Jamie exclaimed. "The other one! The one filling the toppings bins in the back."

"How could we miss him?" said Kelley. "He looked like Nick Jonas."

"Is that a good thing?" asked Sara.

"Yes!!" Jamie and Kelley screamed at the same time.

"Do you think he has a girlfriend?" asked Kelley.

"I don't know," said Sara, "but he was totally looking at you."

"No way," said Kelley, her cheeks a bright red."

"Not to be a buzz kill," said Sara, "but we are all wearing matching pink and black track suits. *Everyone* in the mall was looking at us."

Jamie laughed so hard she almost snorted her frozen yogurt out of her nose. She had to stop and catch her breath.

"Oh my god, Sara, you're hilarious," Jamie exclaimed. "And your vault today was *amazing!* Lightning fast and beautiful."

"Are you saying that because my lip is torn up?"

"No," Jamie answered. "I'm saying that because I'm *jealous*. Can you maybe walk me through it a bit tomorrow before practice?"

Sara smiled a genuine big smile.

"Sure can," she said. "You've almost got it anyway."

Jamie tossed her empty yogurt container in a nearby trashcan and squeezed herself between Kelley and Sara, linking arms.

"Bye boys," she called over her shoulder.

All three girls skipped Wizard-of-Oz-style down the street laughing and giggling.

Judi watched her girls proudly.

Maybe they'd pull together in time for Regionals after all.

CHAPTER 9: SARA COACHES

Jamie ran toward the horse, knees bent, arms pumping.

"Faster," called Sara, "Use your arms!"

True to her word, Sara had gotten to practice early to help Jamie with the dreaded Piked Tsuk. Jamie imaged the Tsuk as a kind of hooded Darth Vader. She was a Jedi knight and Sara was Obi Won teaching her how to channel the force.

"Spring up!" Sara called.

Jamie hit the springboard and pushed her feet against it propelling herself into the air. She kept her body straight and rotated slightly so that both hands hit the horse sideways. She rotated again until she was facing the horse and then moved away from it. Her goal was to land facing it.

"Now turn!" Sara cried. "Turn!"

The floor came up to meet her fast. Too fast. Jamie landed on her feet without doing a single pike, her body leading forward. She'd had way too much momentum. She fell to her knees.

"ARRRGH!!" Jamie shrieked. She looked up toward the ceiling and cried out in frustration like someone in an old gladiator movie.

Some of the younger recreational girls looked over to see what was up.

Jamie waved to them, a little embarrassed.

"Think about standing up in the air and spotting the wall before you tuck," Sara said. It was the same pointer Judi had given her, but Sara used different words to explain it and that seemed to help Jamie.

"Try again," Sara said patiently.

Jamie noticed that Sara didn't lick her lip or bite the inside of her cheek once while she was coaching her.

She could almost hear a *DING* go off inside her head. She made a mental note to talk to Judi about her idea after practice.

Jamie tried again and ended up slamming into the mat on the other side of the horse.

"Well, at least you got over," Sara said.

Jamie shrieked.

"Chill," said Bethany, as she sleepily leaned down into a calf stretch. "I heard you from all the way inside the locker room."

"Well?" Jamie cried. "What if I *never* get it? What if I have to stay at level 7 forever? What if--what if I turn sixteen and I'm still a level 7 and I can never compete at Regionals or Nationals or or—".

She couldn't quite bring herself to say, "The Olympics." It was everyone's dream.

Just hearing the note of panic in Jamie's voice was more than Bethany could handle. She could barely deal with her own fears.

"Um, yeah," she said vaguely and sought out the calm intensity of Nadia.

Sara stretched out an arm to Jamie to help her up.

"Again," she said.

Nadia and Bethany stretched out as Jamie ran through the vault a few more times with Sara. Kelley wasn't there yet.

Judi consulted with Max in her office. They'd be cycling through each of their floor routines later in the afternoon and she would need his help.

Even through their training, Jamie and Sara couldn't help but overhear snippets of Nadia and Bethany's conversation. They weren't even trying to keep their voices down.

"Not serious. Not serious at all."

"Totally bringing us down."

"It's not like cramming for a test. You can't do it all the night before."

"Well, you can, but you can't *win* that way."

"Doesn't she realize we're a *team*. Everyone's score counts."

"Kelley's going to bring us all down."

Jamie had had enough. She knew for a fact that Kelley wasn't late to practice because she had a game or a dance class. She was late because her shoulders hurt so badly her mom had to take her to the physiotherapist.

Jamie had been up late the night before e-chatting with Kelley about it.

We're a team and Kelley is in pain, Jamie thought. *Nadia and Bethany are just being gossipy little backstabbers.*

All the anger and frustration Jamie had been feeling lately bubbled up inside her at once. Frustration about her grandma being in the hospital, about being far away from her friends in Miami who knew her as more than just a gymnast, all the pressure to nail this vault and the feeling of utter powerless that she couldn't just make it happen—it was all too much to keep inside.

Sara must have read her facial expression, because she took a step backward, clearing a path for Jamie.

Jamie marched right over to Nadia and Bethany.

"What are you two talking about?" She demanded. "Or should I say *who?* I'm tired of all this gossiping."

"We were just noticing that our dear teammate Kelley is missing *yet* another practice," said Nadia calmly, locking eyes with Jamie. It was a clear challenge and Jamie was not going to back down.

To Sara, Jamie and Nadia looked like two dogs circling each other before a fight. She fidgeted with the zipper on her hoodie but did her best not to move it. She bit her upper lip instead.

"Well, what is this like the third practice she's missed this week?" asked Bethany. "I thought your friend had renewed her commitment to gymnastics?"

"*MY* friend?!" shouted Jamie, outraged. "Since when is Kelley just *my* friend? How can you talk about her like that? She's our teammate."

"Some teammate," said Nadia coldly. "Her need to put dance or whatever the activity-of-the-week is above gymnastics is bringing the whole team down. You're only as strong as your weakest link."

"You think Kelley is a weak link?" asked Jamie, not backing down. "She's been practicing all week with sore shoulders and she hasn't said a word. She's at physio right now."

Jamie felt the pressure inside her pulsing like raging water battering against a damn. A tiny voice in the back of her head told her to calm down, to take a deep breath, that she was just taking out her anger about other things on Nadia. She knew she was about to cross some invisible line, but she wanted to cross it. She wanted all the pressure to go away.

Her body trembled and she felt the tears start to run down her cheeks.

Then Jamie exploded.

"Kelley is *our* friend," she said. "*Friends* support one another no matter *what* their decisions. If our *friend* Kelley wants to do gym and play soccer and dance in a bear suit outside H&M...if she wants to learn Russian while playing the violin underwater, then that is her *choice* and as her *friends*, we have to support her." Jamie was panting with rage.

She settled down a bit and asked, "Why are you so bothered by it anyway?"

Nadia stared at her defiantly while Bethany avoided making eye contact.

Sara was stunned. She'd never seen Jamie have a meltdown before. It was impressive.

"Dude, what are you guys screaming about?" Kelley had walked in mid-argument. She shook the raindrops off her jacket and looked around confused.

"What's going on?"

Jamie was full-on crying now.

Bethany turned to Kelley, half-panicked, half-excited to see what would happen next. Sara put a pre-emptive hand on Kelley's shoulder.

Nadia continued talking as if she hadn't noticed her audience.

"Why am I bothered?" Nadia asked. "Because *I* take gymnastics seriously. It's all I have—the only thing I've been working towards. So why should a kid who is a year younger and great at everything waltz in here without even working hard and have the chance to knock me off the podium?"

Nadia didn't raise her voice. She kept it even keel, but it grew more and more cutting with every word.

"You wanna talk about a *real friend?*" she continued. "If Kelley were a *real friend* she'd make a commitment or walk away and let those of us who are serious and dedicated have a shot at our dreams. That what a *real friend* would do."

For the first time since she moved to Bellevue, Jamie realized Nadia had been stressed, too—that all of her snobby silences and efforts to out-do everyone else were about her own fears. But it was too late for empathy. Jamie's whole body quivered from the confrontation.

Jamie and Nadia locked each other in a stare, each daring the other to look away first.

Kelley dropped her gym bag to the ground, trying to make sense of what was going on. Had they been arguing about *her?*

Beside her, Sara licked her top lip, once, twice, three times and rocked slightly back and forth. All the fighting and the pressure to control her own ticks was too much. She ran her fingers through her long black hair, soothed by its silky feel between her fingers.

"Guys," said Bethany in a soft voice. She walked forward to stand behind Nadia. It was subtle, but to Kelley, her friend had clearly chosen a side.

Kelley felt like she might break. Tears streamed down her cheeks. She hadn't skipped practice. She'd been at the doctor. For an injury she probably never would have gotten if she'd kept up with her dance workouts. Workouts she had skipped in order to train for a competition she might not even be allowed to compete in.

The injustice hit her like a hundred pound weight.

Without saying a word, Kelley turned and ran to the locker room, her injured shoulder shuddering with convulsive sobs.

Sara quickly followed her, happy for the escape.

Jamie gave Nadia one more menacing glare and headed to the locker room herself.

"God, they are too much," Bethany huffed as if the entire display was orchestrated to cut into her own personal training time. "Can't we just workout without drama for ONE day?!"

Nadia shot her a look, but didn't say what she was thinking. Instead, she headed to the mats to finish her cool down and stretch.

Judi walked out onto the floor to see Bethany stomp off toward the vending machines.

The Bellevue Kips were a team divided.

So much for frozen yogurt solving everything, Jamie thought

CHAPTER 10: LOSS OF FOCUS

"Focus Jamie," Sara coached. "I know you're sad about your grandma, but you've got to find a way to keep your mind clear in the gym."

"What? Oh, okay," said Jamie. For the second day straight, Sara had come to practice early to help Jamie with her vault.

"Look, Jamie," Sara said. "I envy you. You're not scared and that's great. It means there's nothing holding you back. The vault is just something hard you have to keep trying until you get it."

That afternoon in the gym was a lot like the day before except for the ginormous wall of silence that had settled between the two factions: the "serious" and "the slightly less serious."

While Jamie worked with Sara, Kelley practiced her vault with Judi. It wasn't flawless but it was getting there.

The more "serious" girls were running conditioning drills with Max and practicing acrobatics for their floor routines.

Today's the day, Jamie thought. *I have to nail this vault or Judi will never let me compete at Regionals.*

"Okay, Jamie," said Sara. "Let's try it again."

Jamie took her starting position. She'd been over this vault so many times, she couldn't stand thinking about it anymore.

Whatever, she thought. *If I can't compete, I'll just join the circus.*

"Yes, that's it, pump those arms!" Sara called. "Spring up!"

Jamie hadn't even realized she'd started running. Her body was on autopilot.

She hit the springboard and bounced up.

"Yes, push off the horse!" Sara cried.

Jamie pushed against the vault with her hands, launching herself into the air.

"NOW!" shouted Sara. "Twist!"

Jamie's body twisted.

"Pike!"

It bent in half at the waist as she rolled forward in the air. Once. Twice.

Jamie hit the mat feet first. She bent at the knees to absorb the impact.

Steadying herself, she raised her arms above her head and smiled.

Seven seconds of pure exhilaration.

She tried to catch her breath.

Seven seconds. That's all it took, but Jamie felt like she'd crossed over some invisible threshold. She could do the level eight compulsory vault! There was no going back.

"Wheeeeeeee!" Sara squealed.

"Whoo-hoo!" Kelley called as she ran over to hug Jamie. They held each other's arms and jumped up and down.

"You did it!" Sara shouted.

"Yes!" Jamie gave Sara a big hug that clearly made Sara uncomfortable.

"I did! It's like it just...*clicked*...like I'd known all along, but just now I *knew* I knew. You know?"

Sara and Kelley laughed.

On the other side of the gym, Bethany turned away from Max to watch the celebration. Jamie's cheers instantly put her in a grumpy mood. It's not like she wanted Jamie to fail, but she knew that if Jamie couldn't do the vault she'd have a better chance of winning a medal herself.

Before Jamie moved to Bellevue, Bethany had been second-best to Nadia. Now, she struggled to hold on to third.

"Can you keep it down over there, please?" she snapped. "Some of us are trying to focus."

Jamie ignored her.

"Nice work," Judi said. "Now do it again. The repetition will aid muscle memory."

Jamie performed the vault again and again and it improved slightly each time. It had taken a lot of hard work, but once she had it, she was *good* at it. While the other girls continued to struggle, Jamie looked like she'd been born to Tsuk.

As the squad transitioned to bars, Nadia gave Jamie an awkward pat on the back as if accepting her into the group of "serious" girls—the real competitors.

"Nice vault," she said as she chalked up her hands for bars.

Jamie couldn't help but laugh. Somehow things were okay with them again—as if Jamie had proven her commitment by mastering an event.

"Thank you," she said as she slipped on her grips.

****

"Okay, ladies, today, we're working compulsory elements on bar," Judi announced. "I want to see everyone do a hiccup from low to high."

Before Sara's accident—before she broke both wrists flipping backwards on the beach—before the fear settled in and the OCD took over, bars were her event. She approached them aggressively and flew through the air with no fear. She still remembered the feeling of spinning and swinging her lithe body from one bar to the next as though it was nothing—as if she were flying. She'd been invincible.

She'd loved that feeling. And she wanted it back.

Now, she carried a constant anxiety around with her—a knot in her stomach, a dryness in her mouth and a racing heart in her chest. She saw it in the slight tremor of her hands and the small bald spot at the base of her neck where she'd tugged and twirled her hair until some of it had fallen out.

Before the State finals, she had washed her hands obsessively so many times; they'd grown chapped and raw. The skin on her palms broke easily when she swung on the bars.

It's not like she thought she could wash away all her new fears and anxieties. Not really.

But what if she could?

The physical act of running her hands under the water felt soothing. And the idea that maybe, *maybe* by washing her hands again everything would turn out okay was enough to keep her doing it. It felt like a built-in good luck charm.

Sara shook off all these thoughts as she stretched out her arms and legs. She pulled the straps on her grips tighter with her teeth.

No fear, she told herself. *Yeah, right.*

"Okay, Sara," said Judi. "Please demonstrate."

Sara looked at her coach, horrified.

She can't be serious, she thought.

"I will be right here the whole time to spot you," said Judi. "You won't fall."

Jamie and Kelley exchanged worried glances.

Nadia calmly stepped forward.

"You won't fall if Judi's spotting you," she assured Sara. "Just aim your feet in between the bars and remember to rotate your body at the peak of flight." They'd always a friendship based on giving one another technical pointers.

Sara nodded.

Okay, she thought. *I can do that.*

In competition, a bar routine had to include a certain number and type of elements like a release and flight transition from one bar to the other, a flight element on the same bar, at least two different ways of gripping the bar, and a change of position or direction—like a turning handstand. It required an intense amount of upper body and core strength, not to mention concentration.

Scores were based on the difficulty of the moves, technique and form and deductions were taken for mistakes, bad form, extra swings that didn't lead to another skill—and of course falling. A full point was taken off if you lost your grip on a bar and dropped to the mats below—a lesson Sara had unfortunately learned first-hand during Regionals.

How embarrassing!

"Sara, you may begin," said Judi.

Sara made last-minutes adjustments to the grips on her hands. She hated the way they felt—just one more thing getting in the way. Then she grabbed the low bar with her hands shoulder width apart.

In competition, the lower bar was a little over five and a half feet high and the high bar about eight feet high, but most gymnasts trained on lower bars so they wouldn't get hurt if they fell.

"She looks nervous," Jamie whispered to Kelley.

Sara used momentum to swing up into a kip. She felt the strength in her arms and immediately calmed down. Swinging her body back and angling her butt up into the air, she brought her toes up to rest on the bar between her hands. Her body was bent in half like a squished V.

"Come on Sara," Kelley said under her breath. "I know you can do this."

Just at the moment when Sara's backside swung out in front of her legs, she released her feet, sending them and her straight legs flying up toward the high bar. When her outstretched body formed a diagonal line between the low and high bars, Sara released her hands.

She felt a brief moment of panic. She was free-flying now. There was nothing between her body and the ground.

Quickly, her legs widened into a straddle, she pulled her upper body up behind her.

Jamie and Kelley willed her on from below.

Sara reached out to grab the high bar and complete the transition—her hands were still only about shoulder width apart—but the grips felt strange. They had a wooden dowel running across the palm that was supposed to help her grip the bar, but Sara wasn't used to them and they made it harder to judge the distances.

She felt herself slipping.

She let out a squeal, but Judi was right there, supporting her butt, pushing her up so that Sara was able to get hold of the high bar and continue into a Kip to handstand before she dismounted.

She felt her feet solidly on the ground and breathed out.

Phew, she thought. *That was close.*

Just as she'd done with Jamie, Judi made Sara repeat the hiccup, also known as an uphill, three more times until she performed it confidently and with ease.

Sara dismounted after her third straight hiccup and smiled at her friends.

"I did it!" she cried.

Jamie couldn't remember the last time she'd seen Sara look so confident and proud. She wrapped her in a hug.

"And that hug *was* because I admire you, OCD and all," she said. "You're so strong."

"Thank you! Thank you!" Sara replied.

Even Nadia was impressed. "Nice form," she noted. She took her place beneath the bars and proceeded to perform her own hiccup flawlessly on the first try.

"Gym nerd," Bethany muttered under her breath.

During Jamie's first attempt, she didn't get enough downswing before the release and ended up missing the high bar by a good half inch. She fell to the mats below, gritted her teeth and got up to try again.

She corrected her mistake on her second attempt and by the time she did her third hiccup, Jamie was performing with a grace and acrobatic skill that far surpassed Nadia's.

"She's really going to give me a run for the gold," Nadia commented.

Bethany glared at her. She felt like she'd been slapped. After all of the weeks of training together, Nadia was talking like Bethany wasn't even in the running for gold.

And what? she thought. *I'm suddenly not serious enough anymore?*

Bethany watched Nadia walk over to consult with Jamie with a sinking feeling in her stomach. Once again, she felt like she'd been replaced.

First Kelley, Bethany thought. *Now Nadia. Does that little brat have to steal all my friends?*

By the time it was her turn to try the hiccup, Bethany was fuming and her concentration was shot.

She managed to keep it together on her first two attempts, but on the third hiccup her foot hit the low bar during the transition, an automatic 0.5 deduction.

"AAAAAAAAH!" she screamed. "If the rest of you weren't so

chatty, maybe we could get some focus in here!"

The rest of the squad looked at each other. They hadn't said a word. Judi made a mental note to have a chat with Bethany's mother.

Bethany stormed off to go sulk in the locker room, while her squad mates moved on to beam. No one was really sad to see her go.

"Is it just me?" Kelley asked. "Or are these meltdowns getting old?"

"Old," Nadia confirmed. "Very very old."

****

Half an hour and a lot of stretching later, five sore gymnasts hobbled out to the parking lot.

"All aboard the Sato Express," joked Yeji, Sara's older sister, as Sara, Kelley, and Jamie piled into the family's mini-van. Sara's sister had just gotten her driver's license and was helping her mom out by caravanning her younger brothers and sisters to their extracurricular activities.

"Any excuse to get behind the wheel," Sara joked.

The girls piled in and Sara's sister cranked up the radio. "Gangham Style" exploded in the back seat and the three gymnasts started dancing.

The Sato-Express passed Jamie's house first.

"Thanks for dropping me off," said Jamie, as she pulled off her seatbelt. "It really helps my mom out to not have to leave my grandma alone."

"Anytime," said Yeji. Jamie waved good-bye to her friends and Yeji pulled the mini-van away from the curb.

"It's good to see Jamie so happy," Kelley chirped. "She's been so worried about her grandma."

"She had a good practice," Sara said.

An awkward silence fell between the two girls in the backseat. Kelley noticed that while Sara's lip had healed, she was sitting on her hands more and more, struggling against the urge to perform some form of ritual.

After a few minutes, Sara looked out the window and said, "It really sucks dealing with OCD."

"I bet," said Kelley.

"It's like I feel crazy one minute and fine the next."

"I feel that way and I don't even have OCD!" Kelley said. "I can't imagine."

"Like on bars today…I was so scared and then I was like my old self and then—."

Sara grew quiet and Kelley placed a sympathetic hand on her knee. She didn't know what to say but she wanted to support her friend.

"What's it like?" she asked tentatively.

"They want me to go on meds," Sara continued, sadly. "They said they'd help—like take the edge off or something. Make it easier. But I know they're just going to make me tired. How can I be me and do all the things I love to do if I'm tired all the time?"

Kelley flattened out the wrinkles in her track pants. She wished Jamie were still there. Jamie always seemed to know exactly what to say to make everyone else feel better.

Sara leaned her head against the cool glass of the car window and Kelley gave her knee a squeeze.

"It really sucks," she said. And she meant it. She didn't know what she'd do if she had to choose between feeling tired all the time or being so anxious she ended up hurting herself. Her life was confusing enough. She couldn't even make a decision to cut out an extracurricular activity and stick with it.

She caught a glimpse of her dance studio out the window as Yeji drove by.

"Oh!" she exclaimed startling both Sara and her sister. "Could you guys drop me off here please?"

Yeji scrutinized her via the rearview mirror.

"What's here?" she asked.

"A dance workshop I really need to attend," said Kelley.

Sara gave her a sidelong glance.

Kelley shrugged and Sara smiled sympathetically. Neither one of them was perfect.

"Your call," said Yeji as she unlocked the van doors.

Kelley slipped out of the car and waved good-bye. Just seeing the door to her dance studio made her feel like she could breathe again.

They'd be so happy to see her. Surely someone would give her a ride home.

Suddenly, her cellphone beeped. A text from Jamie.

<<Grandma worse. On way to hospital ☹>>

Kelley's heart sank.

Another situation she didn't know how to handle.

She stared at the screen on her phone, confused.

Hmmm, she thought. *I wonder if they make an emoticon for that.*

CHAPTER 11: CHRISTMAS KIPS

"Deck the halls with boughs of holly," Kelley sang as she waved a candy cane in Jamie's face. "Fa la la la la—"

Jamie wasn't having it.

She let Kelley put a stocking cap on her head, but she could barely manage a smile let alone holiday cheer. It had been a full week since Jamie's grandmother had been admitted to the hospital and she wasn't home yet.

It was beginning to look a lot like she *wouldn't* be home for Christmas.

Only week until Christmas, Jamie thought. *And three weeks until Regionals.*

Instead of keeping an advent calendar to track the days leading up to Christmas, the girls had one that counted down to Regionals. The gymnast with the best performance of the day got to eat the chocolate out of a little cardboard door in their wall calendar. It was one of Judi's coaching strategies—all about incentive.

Nadia had gotten the chocolate for the past week straight. She never ate it and she never shared it.

It was getting on everyone's nerves.

"I think she's storing them up to use in her witch's brew," said Bethany.

"Wrong holiday," said Jamie, trying to muster up a tiny sense of humor.

"I feel like a dog in potty training," Kelley moaned. "I want my treat!" She felt like she had to keep up the Christmas spirit for the whole squad but it was hard work. They were an intense bunch of girls.

Kelley pulled off the top of her tracksuit and stuffed it down into her leotard. "Ho ho ho!" she said, making her belly shake up and down. She leaned in close to Jamie like the deranged Santa from A Christmas Story. "HO. HO. HO," she said, making a silly face. "Ho. Ho. HO!"

Jamie finally cracked.

"Okay, okay," she said, laughing. "You win! I have Christmas spirit."

"Excellent," said Kelley. "I was beginning to think I'd lost my touch."

"You? Lose the ability to make everyone laugh?" said Bethany, sarcastically. "Never."

Kelley wasn't sure if that was a compliment or an insult but she decided not to be offended.

She pulled the tracksuit top out of her leotard and headed for the mats to check on Sara. She'd been a lot quieter in practice since their conversation in the car and, even though her routines were slowly improving, Kelley was worried about her.

Suddenly a bell rang and Judi bounded out of her office wearing a red-and-white sateen jumpsuit that made her look big and round. She even had a fake cottony beard dangling off her ears.

Max was dressed up as Hanukkah Harry from *Saturday Night Live*.

"Um, Max, none of us are Jewish," Bethany pointed out.

"It was that or an elf costume," said Max in his lilting British accent, "and I am no woman's elf. Besides, I'm a quarter Jewish on my father's side. That has to count for something. I like for all holiday traditions to be represented."

"What about Kwaanza?" asked Kelley.

"And Diwali?" asked Judi.

Max slumped his shoulders. "I have failed you all." Then his face melted into a giant smile. He pulled a package out from behind his back.

"I made snowmen cookies."

"Yes!" shouted Bethany as she bounced up off the mat to be the first to grab one. The other girls followed her lead—even Nadia and Jamie.

"HO! HO! HO!" Judi cried, ringing a golden bell. "Merry Christmas! Merry Christmas!"

She pulled down her beard to reveal rosy cheeks, freckles, and a bright mischievous smile.

"Who wants their Secret Santa presents?" she asked.

"I do! I do! I do!" All five girls bounced up and down.

Judi claimed exchanging gifts was all about the holiday spirit, but the girls suspected it was Judi's way of bringing them together as a team before Regionals.

They only had one week of training before the holidays and two weeks afterwards and most of their routines were still off. There wasn't a lot of time for improvement.

Judi pulled out the first gift, wrapped carefully in shiny red and green paper.

She read the name on the card. "Bethany."

Bethany jumped up and tore her package open.

"Ooh, lip gloss!" she exclaimed. "'Berried treasure.' *Tres mois!* From?" she rummaged in the torn paper for the gift tag. "Kelley."

"It's for your floor routine," Kelley said.

"You know me so well, thank you!" Bethany blew Kelley two air kisses. Even the Christmas Spirit couldn't quite get the girls to hug.

Judi pulled another gift out of her bag.

"Jamie." She announced.

Jamie grabbed her gift and quickly pulled off the pink bow and silver paper.

"Sparkly fuchsia, black, and silver nail polish!" she exclaimed. "Thank you…" she quickly scanned the card. *"Bethany!!"*

Jamie jumped up and hugged her squad-mate. Bethany forced a grin.

"Kelley," Judi announced as she handed Kelley a small gift, wrapped in gold paper.

Kelley carefully pulled off the paper. "Tiger Balm?"

Nadia shrugged. "It works."

"Thank you," said Kelley. "It's perfect. I'll use it every day."

Sara opened her gift next—a fuchsia and silver pocket organizer from Max.

"Um, thanks," she said.

An organizer? she thought. *Like—what's he trying to say?*

Judi and Max opened their gifts next to lots of oohs and aahs.

"And last, but certainly not least..." Max announced before biting the head off a snowman.

"Nadia!" Judi finished. Nadia calmly lifted herself off the mat using only the strength in her legs and abs.

She opened her package. It was empty.

She pressed her eyebrows together and frowned.

"Is this supposed some sort of message?" she asked.

"You could at least have given her coal," Bethany commented.

"No! No!" Jamie cried. "Read the card."

Nadia opened a hand-made red-and-silver card. A list of songs was written on it in careful bubbly handwriting."

"Money's tight," said Jamie. "So I made you something."

"You made me a playlist!" Nadia exclaimed. Her golden eyes brightened.

"Uh-huh!" nodded Jamie. She pulled a USB key out of her pocket. "I have it right here. It's warm-up songs."

Nadia paused. "That was really sweet."

Jamie shrugged. "I tried."

Nadia started reading off the list of song titles.

"These are just so...*me.*"

"Have you figured out the pattern?" asked Jamie, as if she could no longer contain the secret.

Kelley, Sara, and Bethany crowded around to read the list. "Pink Floyd, Hava Nagila—."

"Oh my god!" exclaimed Bethany.

"They're all songs from Olympic gold-medal winning floor routines," Sara said.

Jamie smiled proudly. "It's a pretty quirky collection."

"It's perfect," said Nadia as she walked over to hug her friend. "Thank you."

Judi clapped her hands three times to get their attention—a clear sign that it was time to get back to work.

"Don't forget the holidays are not an excuse to pig out," Judi warned them. "Remember, to keep up with your stretching. In fact, it's a good opportunity to cross train. Get some running in, stay in shape for Regionals."

Max stood behind Judi and rolled his eyes.

"Of course, they're going to stay in shape," he said. "They're athletes, competitors, winners, gold—"

Jamie's cellphone let out a round of dogs barking "Jingle Bells," interrupting Max's speech.

Judi frowned until she realized she'd made an exception to her no-cellphones-on- the-floor rule so that Jamie could receive updates about her grandma.

Jamie looked panic stricken.

Nadia gripped her hand.

The girls gathered around her for support as she slid her forefinger across the phone's screen.

"My *abuela's* coming home!" she shrieked. "She's going to be home for Christmas Eve! Her face lit up and all five girls jumped up and down. Judi had to plug her ears for protection.

"I'd say that's reason to celebrate!" said Max. "Who wants hot apple cider?!"

CHAPTER 12: BAD MEDICINE

Sara had come home from the Kips's holiday party and immediately shut herself up in her room. She carefully hung her sweater up in the closet and tossed the organizer onto her neatly-made bed.

She glared at her Secret-Santa gift, running a finger along its cool, smooth surface.

Is that what people think of me? she thought. *That all I think about is being in control and what? Studying or something?*

She bit her top lip and threw herself down on the bed. Her bottle of medication stared at her from the nightstand. For two weeks, she'd been exhausted. Her limbs were fatigued and heavy and she felt like she passed every day in a dull but constant fog. The doctors kept telling her she'd get her energy back once her body had had time to adjust, but Sara wasn't so sure.

She was tired. And being tired gave her a whole new list of things to be worried about. She worried that her reflexes wouldn't be fast enough and she'd lose her grip on the high bar. She worried that her balance would be off and that instead of her foot finding the beam after a flip, it would find air and she'd fall to the ground breaking her ankle. She worried that she wouldn't have enough energy to complete a full rotation during her acro-moves on floor and that she'd crash to the mat and break a finger or worse.

She worried that she'd spend the rest of her life worrying and that she'd never feel like herself again.

Maybe I can write all my worries out in my new organizer, she thought bitterly.

Sara had been performing consistently in practices before she went on her meds, but Regionals were only a couple of weeks away and Judi wouldn't be allowed to spot her. Or Sara wouldn't let her. Having a spotter meant an automatic deduction.

Why compete if you were going to start down anyway?

Sara had never been the kind of girl who strove for second best. She wanted to be number one and she didn't see how that was remotely possible in her present state. There were a million and one ways she could get injured during competition. All she had to do was loose focus for a millisecond. And considering she couldn't even *stay* focused for a millisecond, she was in trouble.

I'm SUCH a failure and I haven't even started yet.

Sara made a decision right then and there to stop taking her medicine.

She hid her organizer under her mattress where she wouldn't have to look at it and every day, she tucked a pill into its ziplock pencil-case instead of into her mouth.

Everything was okay at first. Sara got her energy back before the OCD returned. But without school and gym to look forward to and keep her days structured, Sara felt lost. It wasn't like she missed the *work* of school, but she missed knowing where she needed to be and what she needed to be doing every day.

She didn't have the energy to force herself to run or train on her own and, without her meds, the constant urges to touch things or perform small rituals grew stronger and stronger every day.

I'm going to be fighting forever, she thought. *For the rest of her life.*

Her squad-mates called her from time to time, but they were all busy with family and holiday prep. No one really had time to hang out.

No one makes time for me, Sara thought. *I'm just the sick girl no one wants to be around.*

For New Year's Eve, her only plan was to watch the ball drop on TV with her family. After dinner, she retreated to her room to watch *The Nightmare Before Christmas* on her laptop. She could tell Yeji knew something was up and she didn't want to deal with it.

78

What if she says something? she thought. *What if my mom finds out? What if they make me start taking those stupid pills again?*

Sara tasted the metallic tang of blood in her mouth. She'd been chewing on her lip and didn't even realize it.

She rolled herself off the bed and headed to the bathroom to rinse out her mouth. The bathroom was a minefield of OCD temptations—the warm water pulsing from the tap, the light switch that begged to be switched on and off, the hair brush that wanted desperately to be run across her scalp.

Before she knew it, Sara was crying.

I'm so weak, she thought.

She picked up the brush and ran it through her hair. Her breath came in short pulses.

Did that mean she was hyper-ventilating?

No one understands. I'm going to lose all my friends.

Her hands were shaking so badly the brush fell out of her hands.

No one loves me.

As lost as she'd felt for the past week, she wasn't looking forward to going back to school in two days. Just the thought of it made her sick to her stomach—the stress of classes, all the homework, all the studying, all the people who *weren't* her friends.

"Ow!" she cried out. Her heart ached as if it were breaking—or she had gas?

But you don't get gas in your chest and she hadn't eaten anything strange.

Sara didn't know what was happening. She bit her lip, hard this time. She drew blood immediately.

There was something bizarrely satisfying about it—a direct cause and effect. Very easy to understand.

OH my god, she thought. *If I start having tremors now, I'll never be able to compete.*

She felt like she couldn't get enough air.

The bathroom suddenly felt too small. She had to get out. She had to open the window, but she had no strength.

She slunk to the ground.

This is what it feels like to go crazy, she thought. *Her chest heaved up and down.*

Help, she thought. *I'll need help.*

And then she was screaming. Screaming with every last ounce of energy she had. Screaming to be heard over the noises of New Year's Eve.

"Yeji!" she cried. "Yeji!"

CHAPTER 13: ONE LESS COMPETITOR

Nadia was already warming up when Bethany got to gym the next day. Sara used to warm up by walking herself through different Olympians' gold medal floor routines.

Now that Sara wouldn't be training or competing at Regionals, Nadia picked up the ritual in tribute. Before this OCD thing, Sara had been a serious competitor and Nadia appreciated that.

She was sad that her friend was having a hard time but the idea of being so anxious you had a panic attack was unimaginable to Nadia.

The members of the squad had all gotten the call on New Year's Day saying that Sara had been hospitalized after having a full-blown panic attack. They'd all gone to the hospital to visit her.

It was the most awkward experience of Nadia's life. No one knew what to say, Jamie kept making annoying jokes, Kelley paced around the room, and Bethany just talked about herself the whole time.

Nadia had just wanted to run away. The hospital bed, the tubes, the sad sad face Sara made—it was all repulsive. Nadia knew it was silly, but she felt like if she stood too close she might catch whatever it was Sara had. She was grateful when Judi suggested she go get drinks for them from the vending machine.

I would never do that to myself, Nadia thought. *But what if it* wasn't *something Sara had done to herself?*

Just then Bethany rushed by on her way to the locker room, distracting her.

Here comes drama, Nadia thought.

Nadia pushed away all the extra thoughts. She went back to her warm-up, focusing her mind on round-offs, giants, and saltos.

There was a competition to win and it was only a week away.

****

Bethany had been up all night again with growing pains. Her English teacher made her stay after school to talk about how sluggish and irritable she'd been lately. She'd even hinted that Bethany might have her period.

Uck! Bethany thought. *What a-- She should mind her own business.*

The whole encounter had made her late for gym. Bethany waved hello to her friends and headed straight to the locker room to change. Her muscles were a bit stiff after so many days off. She peeled off her jeans and quickly pulled up her black and fuchsia warm-up leotard.

It was tight.

She could barely pull it up over her shoulders and once she did, she had to hunch over a bit to keep it on. It hurt so badly in the crotch, she had to pull it right off. Bethany checked the label.

Everyone had the same color leotard—standard Kip black and fuchsia. Bethany had accidentally tried to put Kelley's on one day right before State finals and had a total freak-out before Jamie forced her to read the name on the label. Kelley was a whole year younger and a full three inches shorter. Of course her leotard didn't fit.

Bethany read the label. No name. Just logo.

Bethany's eyes widened in panic.

She held the leotard up to the light. There were the fuchsia and silver stars, there was the tiny tear from when she'd flubbed a move and fallen off beam.

This was her suit all right.

Bethany felt like gagging.

Regionals are next week, she thought. *I don't have time to adjust to a whole other inch of height. What am I going to do?*

Bethany sank down half-naked onto the cold hard locker-room tiles just as the door swung open.

Jamie was cheerfully singing, "What Makes You Beautiful."

"Could you pick a more lame song?" Bethany snapped.

Jamie, Bethany realized, was her biggest problem. If Jamie hadn't joined the team and stolen her spot on the podium, Bethany could relax a bit about the upcoming competition. She'd have more wiggle room.

Bethany sprang to her feet, practically tripping over a pair of black sweatpants as she struggled to pull them on.

"Do you have to be so chipper all the time?" Bethany snipped.

"Whatever's bothering you," Jamie said calmly. "Don't take it out on me."

Bethany yanked a fuchsia tank top over her head and stormed out of the locker room in a rage, almost knocking Kelley over.

Kelley whirled around to catch her balance. Bethany made a harsh clucking sound with her tongue as if Kelley had purposefully gotten in her way.

Jamie and Kelley stood frozen in the wake of Hurricane Bethany.

"Again with the moody?" Kelley asked.

Jamie shrugged. "Why should today be any different?"

Back out in the gym, Jamie and Kelley ignored Bethany's pouts and sighs.

They had their own problems to deal with.

Judi called them all over to the mat for their traditional pre-workout chat.

Jamie looked around for Sara.

"Is she still in the hospital?" Jamie whispered to Kelley.

"I don't' know," said Kelley. "Maybe she's taking it easy for a little bit longer?"

Bethany caught Nadia silently taking in her black sweatpants and fuchsia tank as if she knew exactly what it meant—an advantage for *her*.

Bethany leaned forward into a deep hamstring stretch to avoid eye contact.

Judi clapped her hands three times.

The girls clapped back.

"Regionals are next week," she announced.

No one seemed surprised or particularly happy to hear the news.

"I'm pleased with where most of you are at and we have a whole week to fine tune," Judi continued. "You should all feel proud. You've done the heavy lifting. Now it's cleaning time."

Kelley raised her hand.

"Is Sara coming?" she asked.

"No," Judi said, in a sad but businesslike tone. "Sara will not be competing with us at Regionals this year." Judi paused to let this information sink in. "Her family has decided to give her a break from gymnastics until the anxiety lessens."

"No!" cried Jamie. "She was getting better."

"Please don't cry," Bethany said, sharply.

"That will be enough, Bethany," said Judi. She turned to Kelley. "Kelley, this means there is a spot for you in the team all-around competition. I trust you still want to compete at Regionals?"

Kelley's cheeks burned as she nodded. She shifted on her bottom awkwardly. She felt everyone's eyes boring into her. She wanted a spot because she was good and because she'd worked hard. Not because her friend got sick.

Jamie placed an empathetic hand on hers.

"Well," said Nadia, breaking the tension. "It's best to keep the drama out of the gym anyway. We can't afford distractions at this level."

She looked pointedly at Bethany. Bethany narrowed her eyes and held Nadia's glare.

Nadia was sad for her friend, but one less gymnast meant extra coaching time and that was always a bonus. *She* didn't break under pressure or feel the need to injure herself in some misguided attempt to win.

Nadia just worked hard.

But would it be hard enough to win?

CHAPTER 14: DIVISION

Bethany alternately stared out the window of the bus and glared at Jamie and Kelley who couldn't seem to stop giggling.

Fine if they want to be besties, she thought, *but do they have to be so obnoxious about it?*

They had a long ride ahead of them. This year's Region 2 gymnastics competitions were being held in Beaverton, Oregon just outside of Portland, which meant a three-hour bus ride.

Three hours was too much time to think about the upcoming competition. There would be three separate training sessions when they arrived tonight and the competitions would begin tomorrow. They were scheduled for the afternoon session with began at noon with a half-hour warm-up.

The athletic center would be filled with gymnasts, coaches and parents from all over The Pacific Northwest.

This year's sponsors included Bethany's favorite energy bar and lip gloss companies as well as Vitamin Water. She wondered if they'd be giving out free samples. At State, they'd gotten a swag bag full of T-shirts, water bottles, a key chain, and a bunch of coupons to local sporting goods stores.

The bus drove over a bump and Bethany bounced up in her seat.

Her stomach tensed.

This could be my last competition, she thought. *My last chance.*

Bethany felt like her own genes were a time bomb waiting to go off inside of her. This could be her last shot at a gold medal in competition. She twisted a random strand of hair between her fingers.

Why couldn't Kelley be the tall one? Tall was good for soccer, wasn't it?

Life, she thought. *It's SO unfair.*

****

The squad's arrival, training sessions, and boring meet-and-greet dinner passed by in a haze.

But the time Judi led them into the auditorium for their warm-up the next day, they were all ready to get the competition over with. Bethany hadn't slept well at all. Usually, she didn't mind sharing a double bed with her mom, but last night her mom had had a restless sleep with lots of kicking and blanket stealing.

As always, the lights in the athletic center added a warm other-worldliness to the competitions. Bethany noticed the smell of musty woodwork and was instantly reminded of their last competition where she'd lost her grip and fallen off the uneven bars.

She took a sip of water and put on her best fake happy face. The center was swarming with other gymnasts, coaches and judges. Bethany felt that appearances mattered—as if you could get a half-point deduction for not looking confident enough.

Judi consulted a schedule she'd been given upon arrival the day before.

"Your first event is vault," she announced.

Figures, thought Bethany.

According to the rules, each girl would have two opportunities to complete the required vault and two chances to complete a vault of their choosing. Bethany wasn't worried about the optional vault. Hers didn't have a high start value, but it was an old reliable. She got through it every time with no major flubs.

But she'd never mastered The Tsuk. Not like Jamie, who never messed it up.

Nadia was up first and flew over the vault without hesitation, completing the piked Tsuk followed by a Yurchenko.

Vault was the event that required the least about of artistry and the most technical skill and it was over before anyone could blink. Nadia's body was muscular and she flew through the air with a strength and technical precision that clearly impressed the judges.

That was easy, she thought. *For Nationals, I'll need to start working on something original.*

She raised her arms high in the air and smiled at the judges.

If I want a vault named after me, she thought, *it will have to be new. Fresh. Something no one's ever done before.*

"I hope I'm that good on vault one day," Jamie whispered to Kelley.

Kelley shrugged.

"You're good now," she said.

"Not yet," said Jamie. "You *are* though."

Kelley shrugged again. "I love vault!" Kelley said, her eyes gleaming. "It's like flying."

"We're so lucky," Jamie said.

"I know, right?" Kelley answered. "I'm up."

Kelley flew through both her required and optional vaults with ease.

She stood between Bethany and Nadia on the sidelines watching the competition as Jamie got ready to perform.

Bethany had her ear buds in and barely acknowledged Kelley as they watched Jamie do a perfect piked Tsuk, but she couldn't help but hear Kelley cheering and clapping when Jamie nailed the vault, outperforming her own practice records.

Unlike Bethany, Kelley was having fun. She'd missed this—the audience, the anticipation, the adrenaline. She felt grateful just to be there.

Almost over, Bethany thought as she took her place at the top of the runway. She was visibly worried. She bit her bottom lip from the stress.

"Break a leg," encouraged Kelley.

"This isn't a dance recital," Bethany snapped.

She took a deep breath and started her run. She knew almost instantly that she wasn't getting enough momentum. So much of vaulting was about all the little things you did pre-flight before you even got to the horse.

Bethany already felt off—clumsy almost.

She tried to make up for the lack of momentum by bouncing extra hard on the springboard, but that just launched her up at the wrong angle. Her palms touched down too far forward on the horse. One of them palms slipped as she pushed off. She didn't fall right away, but she didn't get enough height to rotate. She fought to pull off a twist before landing, but it wasn't a piked Turk. She stepped out on her landing to keep her balance.

Judi ran over to consult before her second attempt.

"I know, I know," Bethany said impatiently, her voice rising. "I knew exactly what I was doing wrong, but I still couldn't correct it."

"Just stay calm and try again," said Judi. "You get one more go."

Bethany took a deep breath to try and calm herself, but she didn't feel calm. She felt like a nervous wreck. And worse than that, she already felt defeated. She tried again, but this time she clipped her foot on the horse during the pike and landed hard on her butt.

It was over.

She could still compete for medals in the other individual events, but she was out of contention for the all-around.

I knew it, she thought. *I KNEW my legs were too long.*

"Bethany, I'm—," Bethany saw Kelley walking toward her with a pained expression on her face and redirected her course straight to the next event—bars. This wasn't about her squad-mates, this was about *her* and she couldn't deal with their concern at the moment.

God, she thought. *It's like all they think about is how it affects them.*

"Save it," she snapped. She blew by Kelley, clipping her shoulder as she passed.

"Are you kidding me?!" Kelley shouted. She was used to Bethany's moodiness and she was used to Bethany getting snippier and snippier as they got closer to competition, but Kelley couldn't deal with it anymore.

She felt good after her vault, but she was still nervous. Bars had always been Sara's strength. At Optionals, Kelley had gone in with no expectations whatsoever and she'd come out with a medal, but now that she'd succeeded once she wanted to do it again.

And she wanted to do it for Sara.

She'd asked Judi to help her incorporate some of Sara's moves into her routine, since the routine Kelley did for Optionals wasn't as technically difficult as that of the other girls.

She swung her arms in wide circles to loosen up her shoulders. Even though it only lasted for about seven seconds, they'd taken a pounding on vault. They already ached and that pain slowly wore away at her confidence.

Bethany's crabbiness was just making everything ten times more stressful.

"I've had enough of you taking your bad moods out on me," Kelley said. "I'm trying to focus on the competition."

"*You've* had enough?" Bethany said, cuttingly. "I'm the one who's had to put up with your constant whining about missing dance class and you and little-miss-sunshine giggling all the time! How am I supposed to focus through all of that?"

"Is that what this is about?" asked Kelley. "You're jealous that I'm friends with Jamie? You don't even act like a friend anymore."

"You're such a stuck-up, spoiled little brat," Bethany shot back.

"Little?!" Kelley squeaked.

"Yeah, little," said Bethany. "It's a wonder you can even reach from one bar to another."

"Girls!" Judi's angry-voice snapped them all to attention. "I will not have arguing on the gym floor. Pull it together."

Kelley and Bethany turned in opposite directions and tried to focus themselves.

Kelley strapped on her grips and took a deep breath while Bethany chalked up her palms.

Jamie reached over and squeezed Kelley's hand.

"Hey, you do how you do," said Jamie.

Nadia walked over calmly with the same perfect posture and unshakable demeanor as always. A little burst of fear shot through Kelley's heart, followed by embarrassment.

Not now, Kelley thought. This was her teammate and she was afraid to talk to her before an event.

Nadia stared Kelley down.

Then her face softened into a warm smile.

"A gymnastics career is too short to waste worrying," she encouraged. "You're excellent at bars. Don't let Bethany psyche you out."

Jamie smiled at Nadia's advice. "Nadia's right," she said. "As usual. Now get out there and have fun. Throw in an extra loop-de-loop for me."

"Is that a new technical term?" joked Kelley. "I like the sound of it. Bellevue Kips on three?"

Nadia looked at Kelley confused, but Jamie stuck her hand out palm down between them.

"Hey, Bethany!" she commanded, "Get your cranky butt over here."

Bethany rolled her eyes and turned away. Then she turned back. Reluctantly, she walked over and joined her squad-mates. Kelley and Nadia stuck their hands on top of Jamie's.

"One," said Kelley, smiling widely.

"Two," said Jamie. Bethany half-heartedly put her hand on top of Nadia's. Nadia caught her eye and shrugged.

"We're like a soccer team now," she joked. She winked at Kelley to show there were no hard feelings.

"Three," Bethany mumbled.

"What?" asked Jamie.

"Three!" Bethany shouted.

"Go Bellevue Kips!" The girls shouted.

"Aggressive and fearless," said Nadia as she patted Kelley on the back. "Now go out there and win that silver!" Kelley's shot her a blank look.

"What?" asked Nadia. "Do you think I'm going to concede the gold? You'll have to fight for that."

CHAPTER 15: UNEVEN AND CLEAN

Kelley stood below the uneven bars and looked up. Even the low bar was high. Judi came over to give her last-minute pointers.

"How do you feel?" she asked.

"Ready to fly," said Kelley with a smile.

"That's what I want to hear," said Judi. "You're strong Kelley. Remember to go for the extra height on your release moves—but only if you're shoulders aren't feeling strained. It's not worth pealing."

"Or face-planting," Kelley grinned.

Judi moved off the mat and crouched down on the sidelines, ready to run in and spot Kelley if she looked like she was going to fall.

Unfortunately, she'd had to be speedy during the past two competitions for both Sara and Bethany.

The judges gave Kelley the go-ahead and Kelley nodded to show them she was ready.

She ran down the mat, bounced once on the springboard and launched herself up to the high bar.

I bet no one else is starting like that, she thought.

Her routine included a bunch of hard high-flying release and catch tricks and a lot of innovative combinations. Her shoulders hurt, but that didn't stop her from flowing beautifully from one move to the next without pauses.

"Oh my god," Jamie whispered. "She's nailing it."

"Mmm-hmm," Nadia mumbled. She was all into enjoying the

experience, but that didn't mean she'd lost her competitive spirit. She studied Kelley's performance, her brain working rapid-fire to see if she'd have adjust her own routine to outperform her.

Kelley maintained tight form and straight bodylines on all her swings.

She's so tiny, Bethany thought. *She looks like she weighs nothing at all.*

Kelley did her required pirouette—a handstand on the high bar that changed directions with a twist—before swinging down to the low bar. Her body was perfectly vertical—not even a hair out of place. Back up to the high bar and swing, swing, swing.

Kelley swung her body up and into a handstand, released at the top of the movement, twisted her body in the air, legs straight and re-grabbed the bar facing in the opposite direction. Her shoulders hurt so bad, she thought she might lose her grip, but she found that if she kept moving, she was really okay.

Sara had had her own original style on bars. Although Kelley could incorporate some of her combinations, she had to make the moves her own. Luckily, she'd had a lot of experience doing that in dance. She couldn't explain how she did it, but the way she moved was uniquely Kelley.

Kelley added an extra pirouette and changed direction with a twist in the handstand position, then she flowed right into a release move and down to the low bar.

She felt energized. In the background, she could hear some silly song from someone else's floor routine. There was something funny about it that made her smile and the smile gave her energy—like music always did. Kelley felt even more exhilarated than she did even during a winning streak in soccer.

She swung once around the low bar, released her grip and transitioned to the high bar. She swung her muscular body around it for momentum. At the top, she stretched her legs into a wide split and then grabbed the bar again with her hands between her open legs.

"Whoa, look at that height!" said Jamie. She was so excited to be competing with her friend again. She'd missed her so much at State.

Even Bethany couldn't help but be impressed.

"I haven't spotted a single deduction so far," said Nadia, struggling to find the right balance between happy for her friend and competitive with herself.

Kelley re-gripped the bar with no problem. She barely paused between her last kip and the dismount. She swung around the bar once twice three times and then twisted her body in the air, her arms crossed over her chest.

She landed with her feet together. No wobble. No step-out.

She felt like she was encased in a little bubble of perfect happiness.

Her friends shrieked and clapped.

Kelley was an undeniably amazing performer. It had been exhilarating to watch her fly through the air. Her squad-mates ran over and enveloped her in a group hug, chattering away about how amazing her routine had been, until Judi walked over and led them all off the mats.

Nadia was up next and her routine was nearly as flawless as Kelley's with a slightly higher start value. It would be a close call.

Nadia had thrown in an extra flight element about halfway through to make her routine even more technically difficult

Judi hated when she did that.

Jamie and Bethany both had solid performances on bars—though Bethany seemed to have lost her spark, that extra bit of energy that she usually brought to each routine.

Once they'd all cycled through bars, the Kips gathered up their things and waited for their scores.

Some overly-excited girl from Portland placed first. Nadia came in second, which was not surprising. The judges loved her. It was like she was born into gymnastics royalty or something.

But Kelley placed first.

Jamie hugged her so hard, Kelley thought she might break a rib.

Then, Jamie turned to the rest of the squad with nervous excitement.

"Who's ready for beam?" she asked.

"Oh, I am!" said Bethany sarcastically.

Nadia chastened her with a stern glare.

"You know," she said, "You don't qualify all-around, but you might try to win a gold in an individual event."

"I know," said Bethany.

"Then why don't you try it," Nadia suggested. "You're getting on our nerves."

Bethany's temper flared, then died out just as quickly. Nadia was sometimes too direct, but she was right. Bethany needed to get over herself. Her strongest event, floor, was up next, and she wasn't going to mess that up by being mopey over vault.

She didn't say another word, but the fire came back to her eyes.

Floor was tough. Bethany made it her personal mission to outperform Jamie, who'd come in first during Regionals. She almost pulled it off, too, but there was something off about the emotion in her routine. Bethany was normally able to channel a character and live inside that character's world for the duration of the performance.

Her floor routine was set to classical music and she'd always envisioned herself as a swan rising up out of the ashes. But today's swan seemed a little...well, vindictive. Her movements, her gestures were too harsh for the soft hopefulness of the music.

She performed all of her acro moves with technical precision and energy, but there was just something not quite right about her dance movements.

Kelley thought what was not quite right was her attitude.

Jamie, on the other hand, was fun to watch. Her routine was genuinely exuberant. And the extra tumbling pass with two saltos—roundoff, whipback, back handspring, full—Max had added to fulfill the compulsory requirements were killer.

Jamie's mom and grandma were seated close to the front row for this event and Jamie thought she pick out their voices among the cheering crowd. She was so excited to see her grandmother in the stands—not quite as strong as normal, but stronger than she'd been in a long time—that she added an extra kick to every move she made.

Kelley had watched Jamie perform her floor routine so many times lately—including her gold medal performance at Optionals—that she had a hard time believing Jamie could improve, but she did. Her kicks were higher, her landings cleaner.

"Holy—," said Nadia, breaking her cool for a minute. "So that's what artistry looks like."

Bethany crossed her arms over her chest and set her jaw firm. She wasn't ready to be a good teammate yet. She was feeling too many things at once and it was all very confusing.

Jamie bounded off the mat and embraced Kelley and Nadia. Bethany managed a curt, "Nice job."

Sara ran down from the stands and hugged her friends.

"Sara!" Jamie squealed. "You came!"

"*Ach du leiber Gott!*" exclaimed Sara. "I think that means Oh my god, in German. I don't remember. You guys are amazing!" She was wearing traditional team colors of fuchsia, black, and silver. She seemed a little more subdued than usual but otherwise okay.

"I've got team spirit," she cheered jokingly. "Yes, I do."

Jamie gave her a giant hug.

"We're so glad you're here," said Kelley.

"Yeah," added Jamie, "we miss you."

"I have to go back to the stands before they spot me and kick me off the floor," Sara said looking around. "Only coaches and competitors allowed down here. But I wanted to tell you how amazing you all are and wish you luck on the rest of the competition."

"Not so fast," said Judi.

Sara froze in place. *Caught!*

But Judi wasn't angry. She looped a VIP badge over Sara's head. Sara looked at it surprised.

"Assistant coach?" she gasped. Her eyes lit up.

"You've earned it," said Judi. "You helped Jamie with that vault and I know you've been giving Kelley pointers on bar." Sara's eyes welled up with tears.

"You're a smart girl and a talented gymnast, Sara," said Judi. She placed a hand on Sara's shoulder. "And this month we've discovered, you're also an exceptionally patient and gifted teacher."

Sara didn't know what to say. All her friends were staring at her.

"Okay, crew," she said. "What's left? Beam?"

Nadia nodded.

"Well then," she said. "Let's get over there and kick some butt!"

CHAPTER 16: BALANCED TO WIN

Nadia and Jamie eyed each other as they stretched out before beam.

"You're going down," Jamie joked.

"Not a chance, Newbie," Nadia shot back with a smile.

They shook hands.

"May the best gymnast win," said Jamie.

"I look forward to seeing the top of your head from the podium," Nadia joked.

"Hey, hey, now," interrupted Kelley. "Not so fast. Bethany and I are out for gold, too.

Bethany smiled.

"That's right," she said. "If you want that medal, you'll have to outshine us first."

Kelley winked at Bethany and for the first time all day, Bethany seemed to be at ease. She was annoyed that Jamie had beaten her on floor, but Jamie's performance was undeniably better. Bethany had let her bitter feelings get in the way and she knew it.

She'd feel bad about it later. She had one more chance to medal and she wasn't going to ruin this one by being stuck up or grumpy.

"Remember what we worked on in practice," Sara told the squad. "Bethany, keep your butt tucked in. Your power comes you're your core. Jamie and Kelley, squeeze tight and tall. Nadia, just do your thing."

"Don't I always?" Nadia joked.

As the girls warmed up, a small blonde girl with thick glasses held on with a sports strap brushed past them on her way to the beam.

"Hello, hello Kips!" she squeaked. "Good luck!"

"Hey, isn't that the girl from the State finals?" Jamie asked.

"The one who tried to psyche us out by telling us what percentage of girls drop out of gymnastics from injury or too much pressure?" Sara clarified bitterly. "Yes."

"Isn't she only like eight years old?" Bethany asked.

"Look at her go," said Kelley.

For a few minutes the girls stopped breathing.

She was only eight years old, but she looked like she'd been practicing gymnastics every second of her life since birth.

"She's so—tiny," said Bethany.

"Of course that's what you notice," Nadia teased. "Did you see the height she got on that back handspring step-out?"

"She's excellent," said Jamie, her voice dropping.

At that moment, the girl did a switch leap, followed by a wolf jump tuck quarter. Starting from a still standing position with her feet together and arms at her sides, the girl raised her arms out in front of her then pulled them back behind her for momentum as she jumped up a good three feet off the beam. At the same time she brought her arms down to meet her legs, she bent and tucked in her right leg while getting full extension on her left, her upper body and arms folding over to meet her legs.

She landed cleanly with her legs together and raised her arms above her head.

"Nice wolf jump," said Nadia.

"Ooh, look at her split leap split jump!" said Jamie. "She has so much power."

"I've never seen a split leap look that beautiful before," said Bethany.

"It's so basic, but she makes it look so…fresh," added Sara.

For her connector, the girl did a cartwheel round off. Later, she added a back handspring.

Her height was unbelievable.

"I can't believe she finds her footing every time," said Sara.

But what Nadia couldn't stop looking at was the way the girl moved her arms. The girl's movements made Nadia want to raise her own arms and move them through the air in the same way. They were beautiful.

This, Nadia, realized was why artistry was important and suddenly she wanted it as much as she'd ever wanted to nail a more difficult dismount or a harder tumbling pass.

That's what I need to win, she thought. *That's what I need...to be balanced.*

The girl with glasses did a front pike dismount, landing lightly on the mat as if she were half fairy.

The Kips all burst into applause.

"We're not winning gold on this one," said Kelley. "Are we?"

Nadia strode toward the beam her arms almost floating by her sides.

"Don't be so sure."

CHAPTER 17: REALISTIC GOALS

"*Abuela*, what do you think?" Jamie asked.

Jamie's grandma sat in a fluffy armchair in the corner of Jamie's bedroom with her feet propped up while Jamie and her mom taped the edges of the walls so they could paint them later that afternoon.

Jamie was in her room with her mom and *abuela* prepping it for Project Redecoration—a reward for working hard and maintaining good grades while excelling at gymnastics.

It had been a rough few months for all of them and it felt good to work on a project together.

"I think we should hang each of your medals up on its own peg, *mi princesa,*" her grandmother said.

"A gold in all-around *and* floor," her mom said. "I'm so proud."

Jamie smiled and wrapped her arms around her mom's waist.

"What can I say?" said Jamie, dramatically. "It must run in the family!"

"*Que lista eres,*" said her grandmother. "So clever. I'll have to be careful around this one."

Jamie pulled away and held up two paint chips, one fuchsia, one silver.

"Now, about the color for the walls," she said. "I'm thinking fuschia with a black border with silver stars around the ceiling, but *mami* thinks the colors are too intense."

"Your *mami* is a very smart woman," said *Abuela*. "She has a point.

How about a softer, calmer pink or blue, so you can sleep at night, and we'll get lots of fuchsia, black and silver accessories to brighten the room up?"

Jamie thought about it for a moment.

"I'll even teach you to sew pillows so we can make them ourselves," her grandmother said, reaching over to move an unruly curl off Jamie's forehead. It bounded right back into unruliness. "Together," she added.

"Mmm," Jamie pretended to think about it. "Okay!" she exclaimed before collapsing on her grandmother again. She loved to feel the warmth of her grandmother's body, the additional weight she'd put on now that she could eat again. Jamie liked being close enough to see the healthy pink of her grandmother's cheeks. She couldn't get enough.

"*Déjala*, Jamie," fake-scolded her mom. "Let *abuela* breathe." But Jamie could tell her mom was just as happy to have them all together.

"I like the idea of a family project," her mom said, her eyes welling up with tears. "Something we can all work on together to make our home even more of a home."

Jamie looked up at her mom.

"You're such a sap!" she joked. With that, Jamie cranked up the volume on her computer and blasted her favorite playlist.

She winked at her *abuela*.

"Let's get this decorating party started."

****

Bethany lay on her bed frantically searching for information on her laptop.

She twirled a strand of blond hair between her fingers.

Her mom came in and sat down next to her.

"I made you some hot cocoa," she said.

"Thanks." Bethany rolled over and sat up to take a piping hot sip. "Ooh, marshmallows *and* whipped cream. Nice touch."

Her mom gently rubbed her back as Bethany went back to her research.

"Rhythmic gymnastics" her mom read over Bethany's shoulder.

"Yeah, it's not so…fly up over things and spin yourself around," Bethany answered.

Her mom looked at her confused.

"I still love gymnastics," Bethany said, "but, I don't know. It's so stressful. I'm not enjoying the competitions as much anymore."

"What are you saying, honey?" Her mom asked.

"Just…just that I think it's time to be more realistic about my height and prepare a Plan B."

"I like the sound of that. Very rational."

"Here look!" Bethany said, brightening up. She clicked on another window on her desktop

"Cirque de Soleil?" her mom asked. "You mean aerial silks?"

"Oh, yes, but not that one. This one." She clicked on another open tab.

"There's a really cool silks class right here in Bellevue where they teach you to do the types of acrobatics used by performers like in Cirque. Can I try it?"

"You mean like climbing up on a silk rope to the ceiling and flipping around on it?"

"You're the one who put it in my scrapbook."

"I see a summer job in your future," said her mom.

"Is that a yes?"

"I think we can manage it," her mom said.

Bethany smiled and took another creamy sip of cocoa.

"I'm going to talk to Judi about Rhythmic, too," said Bethany. "It's like an extended floor routine with props." Bethany sat up and chattered excitedly, telling her mom all the differences between artistic gymnastics and rhythmic. "I'd get to use hoops and ribbons and batons," she said, "and sometimes you can be out on the mat performing *with* your teammates. Anna Styles from my math class does it. She says it's lots of fun." Bethany was talking so fast her mom could barely follow her.

"I just want to check out all my options before I rule anything out," she concluded. "Nationals are a few months away and I'm not sure I'm ready to count myself out just yet. Plus Rhythmic is an Olympic event, too, so I can still win Olympic gold." Her mom smiled at her.

APRIL ADAMS

"No way I'm giving up that dream," Bethany said, her eyes sparkling.

"Wise, so wise," said her mom. "Dreams are important." She leaned over and kissed Bethany's forehead. "Now, how about you get out of this room and come shopping with me? We have a bronze medal in floor to celebrate."

"Oooh!" Bethany squealed. Then she paused and looked at her mom—her shiny blond hair, her warm green eyes.

"Mom?" she said. "Thanks for being so supportive even when I'm a cranky."

"You're welcome," said her mother. "I appreciate your apology. Do you think you maybe owe your teammates an apology as well?"

"Probably," said Bethany, turning back to her laptop. "But one thing at a time."

****

Kelley's mom tucked her into bed. They both stared at her mounting collection of medals before her mom turned the light out. Kelley had won gold in bars and a bronze on vault. She came in third all-around.

Sara had been so excited during the medal ceremony, she actually cried in public.

Kelley's mom turned off the lights and they both sat together quietly for a minute, letting the excitement of the day wind down.

"Mom," Kelley said. "I've been sneaking off to dance classes."

"I know," said her mom. "I was giving you time to figure things out for yourself before I said anything."

"I'm sorry," said Kelley.

Kelley's mom nodded solemnly.

"Mom?"

"Yes, sweetie?"

"Will you help me figure out how to balance things?" she asked. "I don't think I can do it by myself."

In the darkness, she could see her mom smiling.

"Of course, I will, sweetheart," she said. "Tomorrow, we'll sit down with your father and a calendar and talk about how you can scale back without missing out on stretching or doing anything to hurt yourself."

Kelley sat up and wrapped her arms around her mom's neck.

"You're the best," she whispered in her mom's ear.

"I know," her mom said as Kelley snuggled back under the covers.

"Mom?" Kelley asked.

"Yes, sweetie?"

"Does this mean I'm not going to get grounded for sneaking around?"

"What do you think?"

"That I'm in big trouble."

"Wise," said her mother. "So wise."

****

"Silver," Nadia stated flatly. "A whole lot of silver." Nadia had placed first on beam and second in every other category including all-around."

She sat up on the bathroom counter while her mom washed up before bed. The gold medal hung around her neck, but she held up one of her medals as if it had germs.

Her mother patted her face dry and looked at her daughter.

"No," said her mom trying to sound enthusiastic, "SILVER!"

"First is better than second," said Nadia.

"Well, then you have something to work towards," said her mom.

"Yay, a challenge," said Nadia, sarcastically.

"Know what?" said her mom.

"What?"

"I'm really *really* proud of you."

Nadia rolled her eyes.

"Do you know how difficult it is to place second all-around and first on beam in the entire region?"

Nadia was silent.

"The *entire Pacific Northwest Coast,*" her mom emphasized.

She put both hands on her daughter's shoulders and shook her gently.

Nadia tried hard not to smile.

"I'm not going to stop until I get a smile out of you."

Nadia smiled.

"Nadia," said her mother, more seriously now, "I'm worried about you and I think I owe you an apology."

Nadia was startled. "What? Why?"

"You have won a medal for each event you competed in at against girls from the entire west coast. You placed second all-around and you can't even take a moment to savor the victory. You worked hard. It paid off."

Nadia looked down.

"And—," her mother's voice caught. "And…I'm afraid it's my fault. I'm afraid I've taught you to—I'm afraid I've been living through your victories because I never made it to the Olympics myself…I'm afraid I've ruined gymnastics for you."

Nadia's mother was crying now.

For a second, Nadia felt gripped by panic. She couldn't move. But after a second she wrapped her arms around her mother.

"No," she said. "You've always tried to teach me balance."

She squeezed her mom tighter.

"And you're right," she said, seeing her medals in a new light. "I have five medals from one competition. Five!"

"It's true," said her mother brightening.

"And a full five months to out-do Jamie in the all-around," she added.

Nadia's mom groaned.

"But in the meantime, you know what I think we need?"

"What's that?" asked her mom.

"A spa date followed by pizza and a movie," Nadia answered happily.

"Ooh," said her mother. "I have taught you well. Very wise, my child, very wise."

CHAPTER 18: ON TO NATIONALS

The next gym practice felt a little more chaotic than usual. Everyone was too excited to sit still and too relieved to focus on the inevitable new compulsory elements for Nationals. Sara had joined them and the girls could not stop chatting about their new plans and the highs and lows of the competition.

"Congratulations, Kips," said Judi.

The squad smiled.

"I *said,* congratulations, Kips!" Judi shouted.

"Whoooo!" Jamie cheered. The rest of the girls clapped.

"You call that energy?" Judi tried again. "Congratulations, Kips!"

This time all five girls busted out cheering, hollering and shouting. Judi was a pro at getting all their jittery energy out before a practice.

"Much better," Judi said, satisfied. "I have an announcement. Sara is going to act as assistant coach until she adjusts to her meds and can work on routines herself."

Sara rose to her feet and stood beside Judi as her friends clapped and cheered.

"Now, Sara is going to lead you in the warm up while I go spot the Recreational girls," said Judi.

"Don't expect me to go easy on you," Sara said with a smile.

"Uh-oh," joked Bethany. "I think we're about to get our butts kicked."

Bethany was full of bubbly energy. She'd added both silks training and rhythmic gymnastics to her week and was training to compete in a level 8 Optionals competition in February so she could maybe still go to Nationals with her friends later in the year. She felt like she had options and that gave her a sense of liberty.

"Can you help me with rhythmic, too?" Bethany asked.

Sara just rolled her eyes. "You know I've never touched a ribbon in my life, right?"

"Sounds like you're going to be busy, Bethany," said Kelley. *"With dance."* She gave her friend the "I told-you-so" look.

"Don't rub it in," said Bethany.

"My mom can make an excel chart of your schedule if you want," Kelley joked. "We had to add physio to mine and take out half of the dance classes I've been sneaking off to. But we added a soccer tournament in August."

"You finally fessed up!" Sara said.

"Indeed."

"And your mom was cool with it?" asked Jamie.

"Depends on your definition of cool," said Kelley. "No new anything for the exact number of months I was sneaking around and no Facebook after seven p.m. She was cool enough not to give me extra chores, but I think that's just because they didn't fit into her excel chart."

"Well, I can teach you how to meditate," Sara offered. "I've gotten minorly okay at it."

"Maybe you should teach us all to mediate," Jamie piped up.

Nadia cleared her throat.

"Okay, girls," said Judi. "Nadia also has an announcement."

"More of an idea really," said Nadia.

"This should be good," Bethany teased.

Nadia stood and walked seriously to the front of the mat.

The girls all scooted closer to listen.

Something about Nadia's demeanor commanded respect.

Despite herself, Kelley felt a wiggle of anxiety in her stomach. She wondered if Nadia would ever stop having that effect on her.

"In order to boost our scores in artistry," Nadia began.

Bethany and Kelley exchanged curious looks. Nadia and Sara were the only ones who'd ever struggled with artistry.

"And to avoid any additional injuries," Nadia continued, looking at Kelley. "I think that…"

"Stop dragging it out already!" Bethany whined.

"That Kelley should lead us all in a one-hour of dance for gymnasts every week," Nadia said as fast as she could.

"What?!" Kelley exclaimed.

"If she's willing," Nadia added.

Kelley was shocked. She waited for the bad part to come, but it didn't. Nadia took her place on the mat beside Bethany.

Jamie, of course, broke the silence. "That's a great idea!"

"I'm into it," said Bethany. "Kelley has so much experience to offer us. And I'm not even being sarcastic."

Kelley smiled at her friend.

Bethany mouthed the words, "I'm sorry", and Kelley leaned over and gave her a big hug.

"I can make a weekly playlist," Jamie suggested.

"Oh!" Sara jumped in, "and we should make a video before Nationals like the Olympic swim team did to 'Call Me Maybe',"

Jamie thought it was a great idea. The rest of the squad looked at Sara confused.

"What?" she asked. "You think you're the only ones learning to lighten up?"

"And if we win at Nationals," said Jamie, "we can have a big dance party."

"Why wait for Nationals?" asked Nadia. "We've already earned it."

She clicked the button on Judi's remote control and the playlist Jamie had made Nadia for Christmas blared over the sound system. She wiggled her hips in a surprising display of rhythm.

"Nadia! You've got moves!" Bethany exclaimed. In an instant, all five girls were on their feet dancing.

"We just might be the best squad ever," said Jamie as she slid down to the ground and did the worm.

Bethany did the worm, too, and the entire group clapped and laughed.

"*Might be?*" asked Nadia, as she wrapped an arm around her friend.

"We've already won that competition."

ABOUT THE AUTHOR

April Adams has spent almost as much time upside down as right side up. As a competitive gymnast she led her University of Alabama team to the top of the podium and although her sights were never on the Olympics, after a degree in creative writing , April went as a journalist to the London games. April loves hiking, baking and spending time with her family in Utah.

Made in the USA
Middletown, DE
26 November 2018